BRITAIN'S
GHOSTLY
HERITAGE

Summoning a ghost.

BRITAIN'S GHOSTLY HERITAGE

JOHN WEST

PUBLISHING

Dedicated to the memory of Elliott O'Donnell, Harry Price, Andrew Green, Peter Underwood and Colin Wilson – fellow searchers for the truth.

ACKNOWLEDGEMENTS

Thanks to Rosie Evans for proofreading my original manuscript. Thanks also to Jason Figgis for designing the front cover.

First published 2022 by DB Publishing, an imprint of JMD Media Ltd, Nottingham, United Kingdom.

ISBN 9781780916170

Printed in the UK

CONTENTS

INTRODUCTION

BY STEWART P. EVANS

This is a welcome second helping of ghostly tales of British hauntings from John West, a knowledgeable surveyor of supernatural lore. In these pages, you will read of some well-known spectres and supernatural tales from around Britain, as well as many not so familiar to readers of this literature. The author is a great storyteller, and his tales are enhanced by his deep store of historical knowledge.

I may not believe in ghosts (or do I?), but I have been interested in such tales since I was very young, and now have a formidable library on the subject. I count amongst proponents of these stories some dear friends now passed, including Andrew Green, Peter Underwood, Richard Whittington-Egan, and Colin Wilson. Before I was 12 years of age I was conversant with the controversial case of Borley Rectory (the most haunted house in England), the stories of the haunted manors, mansions, and stately homes of our country. I found that there was nothing quite as nice for bedtime reading as a good ghost book. John asked me if I had a personal story of a haunting that I could share.

Over the years, whenever the opportunity arose on my travels, I would ask family, friends, and others if they knew of any local supposedly haunted houses or ghost stories. And my interest was not confined to allegedly 'true' ghost stories, the fictional tales fascinated me too. I avidly read the works of M. R. James, E. F. Benson, L. T. C. Rolt, Charles Dickens, the Rev. R. H. Barham and many others. It was no wonder that I became interested in the idea of spending a night in a supposedly haunted house.

In 1972 I was approached by a couple of similarly minded friends who mentioned that they would like to spend a night in a haunted location and asked if I knew of somewhere. I replied that I actually did. It would obviously need to be somewhere that was 'available' for such a venture, or should that be adventure? With an established interest in World War Two aviation, and particularly the various derelict airfields in East Anglia, especially Suffolk, I had heard stories that Debach airfield, an ex-American bomber base near Ipswich long abandoned by its wartime inhabitants, was haunted by a soul who had never left his wartime home. It was said that on a misty night an airman, in full flying gear, wandered the lonely field. However, the prospect of a night out at a remote, and probably cold, rural location, did not seem too appealing.

My friends were more interested in a story that my mother had told me many years before about a large manorial lodge located in the haunted marshlands of the Suffolk coast. My mother was convinced of what she had experienced and, ever the sceptic, I preferred to think that perhaps a trick had been played on her. It was in the wartime years when, as a teenager, she had been evacuated to live with a couple who lived at Middleton, near Yoxford, whom I came to know as 'Uncle Stanley and Auntie Ethel'. Stanley was the village blacksmith and he knew many farmers in that part of the world. This, as I remember it, was my mother's story.

Uncle Stanley was very friendly with the caretaker, who lived, with his wife, in the house in question. They sometimes paid a visit to this lonely house with its commanding view across the adjacent countryside. So it was that my mother accompanied 'auntie and uncle' on a visit one evening to see the caretaker. He and his wife occupied the east, or seaward, end of the house and the remainder of the house was untenanted at that time. There was no one else in the building other than my mother and the two couples. They all sat in the ground floor living room which faced out onto the countryside at the front of the house. Above the room they were in there was a long corridor, running from front to rear of the first floor, with doors into a few bedrooms off it. This wing of the house was not connected by a door into the rest of the building. As they sat talking by dim, flickering, lamplight, there came, suddenly, the sound of heavy footfalls along the corridor above in a house that contained no other living souls than themselves. As is the case in so many ancient Suffolk abodes, there was a narrow staircase from the bedroom corridor down to the room they were in, that ended with an old wooden door which opened directly into the room and which was fitted with a Suffolk latch. My mother heard the footsteps descend the stairs and stop abruptly at the door into the room. By now all five of them were staring at the door, waiting for it to open, and for whoever, or whatever, to enter the room. In an instant the caretaker jumped up and ran across to the door, pulling it open. There was no one there. He said that this was not the first time they had experienced this and there was never anyone there.

It is true that such a story is incapable of being proven and that the memory, and truthfulness, of the teller has to be relied upon if any belief is to be attached to it. My mother was not in the habit of telling fanciful tales and I heard this one told by her when others wanted to hear it, and she always attested to its veracity. This was enough for my friends in 1972, it must be true and could we spend a night in the property to see if anything would happen. I knew that the building was unoccupied, and had been for several years. I was friendly with the old gamekeeper and through him the owner of the property was contacted and he kindly granted us permission to spend a night in the house.

Apart from my mother's story, the only other tale I had heard concerning the property was that the ghost of a woman in white had been seen on misty nights on the very long drive leading down to the public road. However, one of my friends had done some research of his own and had tracked down, and spoken with, a noted psychical investigator who lived not too many miles away, Mr G. P. L'Estrange. He had documentation telling the story of a former owner of the house who went mad and used to run around the different floors and rooms of the house with a saddle (but no horse) between his legs. A habit he had been unable to shake off even after death.

The day for our visit was arranged and we duly turned up, in our cars, at the yard of the house, it was still daylight although darkness would soon be creeping in. We felt that a thorough search of the house, attic to cellar, would be in order before we set up for the night. It was about 8pm and we planned to spend the first part of the night in the main house, near the staircase, and then migrate to the room at the east end where my mother had experienced hearing the strange footsteps some 30 years earlier. Midnight sounded like a good time to be in this room. We were armed with torches and a couple of candles for illumination. I have to say that Ted the gamekeeper, whose name graced the pages of the *Guinness Book of Records* for catching the longest known adder, had a well-developed sense of humour and I did not entirely trust him not to 'play the ghost' during the watches of the night.

The search of the house was quite uneventful other than a bat, presumably not hired for the night, which flitted around the attic area. We ended up in the cellar which, we had been told, was utilised in bygone days to lock up a smuggler who had been caught. Just before midnight we ventured into the long drive supposedly haunted by the 'woman in white'. By this time a thick sea mist had settled over the hinterland and visibility was down to a yard or so. We returned from the dank outside to the relative shelter of the 'haunted' room in which we had planned the vigil. We placed a candle on the windowsill and lit it. The thick white mist outside pressed against the glass; of atmosphere there was plenty. Midnight came, passed and nothing untoward occurred. We felt that 30 minutes or so in the room was enough and then we returned to the main entrance hall of the house.

We had earlier placed various 'controls' in this part of the house and these included a few threads placed at strategic points to see if anyone had passed through them. Naturally,

Stewart Evans with Andrew Green.

the external doors were included as we feared that, perhaps, the mischievous gamekeeper might consider giving us a fright. They were in place. However, a thread placed across the bottom of the stairs in the hall had been dislodged. Another search was made of the gloomy cellar with no result. We had decided to call it a day (or should that be 'night'?) at 4am, and that we would pass the remainder of the night in the entrance hall. It was uncomfortable and cold, the only relief being a pile of straw that we could sit on. Throughout the vigil, on odd occasions, we could hear a faint, remote, deep, booming, noise, seemingly emanating from beneath the house. For this we found no explanation. As planned, we packed up at 4am and made our separate ways home.

This story, I should imagine, is typical of many such ghost-hunting nights spent in haunted houses. It was certainly an atmospheric experience, but one not to be recommended to those who favour their creature comforts. It was my first, and last, vigil in a 'haunted house.' It is much more pleasant to curl up with one of John's excellent books and allow him to provide the entertaining and informed telling of the ghostly stories.

Stewart Evans, 2021

Stewart Evans is one of the world's leading experts on Jack the Ripper and has published several books on the subject. He is also the author of a biography of *James Berry, a Victorian hangman*.

FOREWORD

BY JASON FIGGIS

When John West invited me to write a foreword to his second volume of excellent ghost stories and mysteries, titled *Britain's Ghostly Heritage*, I set out thinking: *What am I going to write about?*

As soon as I asked the question, the answer came almost immediately: Timeslips.

I have been thinking a lot recently about the two experiences I have had in this intriguing area – one in the rolling hills of Wiltshire in England, the other in deepest rural Ireland. Both are separated, not just by a body of water but by a decade of time as we normally experience it – on a recognisable trajectory of forward movement.

In the 1990s my then partner Ann Murray and I would travel the length and breadth of Ireland in search of ruins of one romantic kind or other – our guide being Mark Bence Jones's wonderful tome which listed every brick or wall or crumbling edifice in any way associated with Norman conquest, religious settlement or aristocratic pile.

On this particular occasion (unfortunately I can remember neither house nor county) we were in search of a majestic ruin of the stately home variety. As the clouds rolled in however it appeared as though a complete wash-out was on the cards. We determined to seek some local assistance and before long came to a boreen (a narrow country road) that led to a single cottage, nestled within a tree-lined clearing at the farthest end of a decidedly rural cul-de-sac.

Ann parked the car at the midway point of the lane (to avoid issues of turning in a narrow space) and I walked up the gravel track – negotiating numerous pools of muddy water – until I came to the door of the rather drab (but notably atmospheric) and isolated abode. I looked back to the car but could not see it and, with the comfortable assumption that it was no doubt obscured by a bend in the road, I knocked on the door.

It was not long (merely seconds in fact) before the lady of the house appeared and she greeted me with a startled expression, appraising me from boot to face with a rapid darting of her eyes. She stepped back instinctively and I determined to put her at ease. I told her

The Stones of Avebury. (Figgis-West)

of my quest and she relaxed somewhat, inviting me into the kitchen which led directly from the open door. I was startled to note the interior; it was not of the late 20th century but much more in line with the décor of the 1930s or 40s. All at once, I took in the scene.

The woman facing me was dressed in clothes of that same period, as were her two small children – a boy and a girl – who now stood beside her. They too proceeded to take in my decidedly modern dress (bright red casual sports coat and navy ski pants – don't ask). They uttered not a syllable. I glanced to the open fireplace as I became aware of a peripheral movement. An old man sat by the fire on a small wooden stool. He smoked a long stem clay pipe and was wearing a cloth cap, he peered up at me and gestured a physical flourish of greeting.

I was overcome by the strangest sensation of being out of my own time but experienced a simultaneous thrill at the prospect of having entered a rare and unusual place.

The children huddled close to their mother as I posed the question once more. The mother became quite animated, secure no doubt in the proximity of her own and wasted no time in telling me that the house that I was looking for had been burned to the ground *'a few years ago'*.

These words are notable – as you will soon realise. I thanked them for their hospitality and left. I turned back to wave goodbye but the door was already very quietly secured in its mooring (and no doubt bolted shut).

At the car I told Ann of my experience and she rolled her eyes with understandable disbelief but when I checked the date of the conflagration – it was 1922 – not 'a few years ago' but more in the region of 73 years. I have never forgotten the experience and the sense of wonder it filled me with.

In 2011, my wife Bernadette and I took a holiday with her parents, Jenny and Sean Manton in the peaceful Wiltshire town of Calne. Bernadette and I were determined to take as many walks as possible, and on one particularly sunny morning we made our way out of town and soon found a signpost that indicated the direction to Avebury. I was stunned. One of my favourite television shows is the wonderful adaptation of Jeremy Burnham and Trevor Ray's screenplay (and subsequent novelisation) *Children of the Stones* – brought to chilling life by producer/director Peter Graham Scott for the Welsh franchise of ITV – HTV Wales – and filmed during the searing summer of 1976. I had no idea we had chosen to holiday within walking distance of this incredible village – which had served as the location for that very same production. To say that I was excited was an understatement.

We soon set out off-road through the beautiful Wiltshire landscape and before long we arrived at an intersection which was not sign-posted for our destination. Do we take the right fork or the left? The sun created a mirage type effect of shimmer and sparkling light along both of the dusty tracks and soon we noticed the thin figures of an approaching couple. As they became clearer and drew closer, I was overcome by a strange sensation (not unlike the experience in rural Ireland a decade before). Soon they were close enough for me to speak to them and when within a few feet, I asked which road led to Avebury.

Their appearance struck me immediately. They were beautiful in an elfin fashion – a young man and woman, both standing around 5ft 6in height. Their skin was translucent; hers lightly tanned, his bronzed. Both had fine veins running across their cheeks and their eyes sparkled. She did the talking and he silently observed. As she spoke, in a very gentle tone but thick accent – that was almost impenetrable – I noticed that their clothes were handmade, with fine but apparent stitching holding all together. Their shoes were similarly crafted from natural materials and everything about them – the combined effect of shimmering looks, delicately made clothes and strange speak – held me in rapture. It turned out that they had just come from Avebury and we were to take the path from where they had emerged. She smiled broadly at my wife and I and they went slowly on their way. We watched them until they were no longer visible and my wife Bernadette commented on their strange beauty. I agreed and we made our way to the wonderful village of Avebury – set among one of the oldest stone circles known to man.

It was some time later that I came across an article that spoke of the many strange occurrences and timeslips that visitors to Avebury had experienced, not only among the great standing stones, but on the paths leading into the village. Our meeting with the elfin couple shot back with great clarity and it certainly gave pause for thought. I have categorically met no one like them, before or since.

All I can say is that both of these experiences held me in thrall with a sense of otherworldliness that was both unmistakeable and undeniable.

Jason Figgis, Film Director, Dublin 2021

SEARCHING FOR PHANTOMS

'All argument is against it but all belief is for it.' Samuel Johnson on the existence of ghosts.

A poll conducted in 2017 revealed that a third of all Britons believed in the existence of ghosts. I count myself as a believer although I cannot say for certain what I believe them to be. Are they the souls of the dead, recordings or even living people from the past briefly interacting with our own time due to a timeslip? All I can say for certain is that I have met too many people who have seen ghosts to dismiss it all as mere fantasy. I have also experienced things myself, as recounted in my previous book, *Britain's Haunted Heritage,* that I cannot readily explain.

My own interest in ghosts stem from the fact that my mother had several books on the subject which I avidly read as a child. I should also add that I have Celtic/Welsh ancestry on both sides of my family, which I have been told by several psychics makes you more open to psychic phenomena.

Another catalyst in the 1970s was watching the Colin Wilson TV series on the paranormal, *Leap in the Dark,* which fuelled my interest even more. This, in turn, led to me reading his book *The Occult* and numerous books on ghosts by Peter Underwood, Marc Alexander, Elliott O'Donnell and Andrew Green. The rest is history as they say.

One of my earliest memories relating to the supernatural concerns my maternal grandfather. He prided himself on his Welsh ancestry and spoke of seeing a glowing white ball hovering at the top of the stairs. He was a child at the time and his grandfather was dying in an upstairs room. He jumped over the ball and rushed into his grandfather's room. The man was dead. His death had coincided with the appearance of the thing at the top of the stairs. My grandfather spoke of death lights and how it was common in Wales for them to appear when someone was near death. He believed that this is what he saw. He was also a miner in South Wales in the 1930s and often spoke about the ghosts said to haunt the mines – the spirits of those miners who had sadly perished in accidents down the years. These ghosts were said to warn of impending disaster by tapping on the walls of the mine with their picks.

John West. (Jason Figgis)

I also remember an uncle in Lincolnshire who was involved in a terrible motorbike accident. He was rushed to hospital where he passed out. He suddenly found himself running up some stairs in a large building. He instinctively knew that to continue up the stairs would mean that he could never return to his body. He turned back and was revived on the operating table. He later found out that for a few brief seconds he had died while under the knife. He later wondered if his 'soul' had briefly left his body on that day? And would he have really died if he had carried on running up the stairs?

Stories like this intrigued me in my youth and made me determined to solve the mystery of ghosts and life after death. Some 40 years later and I am still looking for the answer!

In this book, you will find another collection of my favourite ghost stories from across the British Isles. Phantom monks and Grey Ladies share pages with mischievous poltergeists and even that arch-fiend of Victorian London, Jack the Ripper! My friend, the film director Jason Figgis has also kindly provided a final chapter devoted to his ghostly experiences in Ireland, a land rich in Celtic mystery and folklore.

Now read on and discover the best of Britain's Ghostly Heritage!

John West 2021
www.johnwestmedia.com

CHAPTER ONE
THE MYSTERY OF JIMMY GARLICK

Some people express surprise to me when I tell them that many churches are reputed to be haunted. But why not? These buildings were the hearts of the community for centuries, standing silent witness as countless souls attended services such as baptisms, weddings and funerals. It is only natural to expect that the intense emotions associated with these events will still echo down the centuries, later to be picked up by those sensitive enough to hear and see psychic phenomena.

One of the most intriguing haunted churches in Britain can be found on Garlick Hill in the heart of old London. It is known as St James Garlickhythe and can trace its origins back to the 12th century. 'Garlickhythe' refers to the nearby landing place, or 'hythe', near where garlic was sold in mediaeval times. The church was destroyed in the Great Fire of 1666 and was rebuilt by Sir Christopher Wren between 1676 and 1682. It was later nicknamed 'Wren's Lantern' due to the profusion of windows.

In 1855 a mummified male corpse was found in the chancel and was placed on display in a glass-panelled coffin for the curious to view upon receipt of a small fee. Theories as to who he could be ranged from a Roman general to the first Lord Mayor of London. Later carbon dating tests carried out for a TV series called *Mummy Autopsy* confirmed that the corpse actually dated from 1641 to 1801. Further tests showed signs of balding, tooth decay and osteoarthritis. The corpse also had pierced ears. Some have suggested that he was a sailor who died at sea, was embalmed on-board, and brought to the church for burial after the ship reached port.

St James's reputation as a haunted church only started after the discovery of the corpse which became known as 'Jimmy Garlick'. Visitors claimed to have felt a presence in the building and it was theorised that the ghost of the mummified man was unhappy about being put on display for a paying public. It is also said that choirboys sometimes carried the mummy around the church in jest, something that can have hardly pleased 'Jimmy'!

The Interior of St James Garlickhythe. (Figgis-West)

Jimmy Garlick. (Figgis-West)   *Peter Underwood. (Figgis-West)*

Researching haunted locations can sometimes be a frustrating experience and 'Jimmy Garlick' is certainly no exception. The haunting has been featured in several books and internet sites devoted to ghosts. However, each account sadly lacks vital information crucial to the investigator. For example, accounts of ghostly activity within the church are given but witnesses are not named and we are left to guess as to the years and months when the phantom was seen. With the passing decades, it can often be impossible to trace the original source material and we are often sadly left with more questions than answers.

All we can say for certain is that the church had a reputation for being haunted, that the mummy was blamed, and that a figure resembling the corpse was alleged to have been seen on several occasions.

In May 1941 a German bomb hit the church, grazed Jimmy's coffin and ended up in the crypt. Fortunately, it did not explode. After this, paranormal activity increased in the church. It is interesting to note that many ghosts seem to become more active after their surroundings are altered or damaged. Is the spirit objecting to the changes or is it simply a recording that has somehow been activated? According to the stone-tape theory, stored residual energy in the fabric of a building is released by alterations to the structure, thereby resulting in a display of increased recorded paranormal activity. This could explain many hauntings but it is still just a theory.

Peter Underwood, renowned ghost hunter and the author of *Haunted London*, records that a fireman during the Blitz spotted a white figure inside the church. The figure ignored his calls to take shelter and vanished upon being approached. On another occasion, the figure, again clad in white, was seen in the nave for a few seconds by a visiting priest.

Another time, a lady visitor was sitting in one of the pews when she noticed, on the north side, a tall figure in white with arms folded. It was gazing intently towards the tower. She turned around to see what the figure was looking at and when she turned back it had gone. She went to the spot where it had been standing but could find nothing.

Mr Underwood also recounts that an American tourist visited the church with her two sons. The older boy suddenly startled his mother by insisting that they leave. He was clearly terrified and claimed that he had looked up the

St James's Garlick Hith.

staircase to the balcony and had seen the figure of a man with his arms crossed. It was covered in something like a white winding-sheet. His face and hands were like that of a dried-up corpse. Neither the boy or the mother knew of the mummy or the stories connected with it. The balcony had been deserted prior to the sudden appearance of the apparition.

Other paranormal activity in the church included the movement of objects, unexplained noises and the appearance of a phantom cat. It is not known if these were connected with the appearance of the 'mummy'.

'Jimmy Garlick' was eventually hidden from view and now lies in a new coffin in the crypt, free from prying eyes. The words on his final resting place read:

'Stop stranger stop as you pass by. As you are now, so once was I. As I am now, so shall you be. So pray prepare to follow me.'

Can it just be a coincidence that the decrease in ghostly activity coincided with the decision to hide 'Jimmy' from view? If so, let us hope that he can finally rest in peace.

CHAPTER TWO
THE HAUNTING OF RATTLESDEN RECTORY

The sleepy village of Rattlesden in Suffolk once laid claim to one of the most bizarre ghost stories in Britain. The scene of the drama was a rambling red-brick rectory, some 500 years old, which stood on a small mound overlooking the river which still snakes through the village. The rectory was long thought by locals to be haunted and one of the passages in the building was even nicknamed 'The Ghost Walk' due to the frequent sound of footsteps heard there at night.

It was during the 1860s that a handyman from Stowmarket was sent one afternoon to the rectory to carry out some repairs. He placed a dust sheet over a pantry door and soon set to work removing some rotten oak panelling.

'As I worked away at the panelling I noticed a sour, musty smell. It was only the ghost of an odour, but it made me feel a shade depressed. Rats suggested themselves to me as an explanation of that smell, for I was told the old woodwork was full of rats.'

He tried to ignore the smell but then started to get the feeling that he was being watched. He even began to imagine that the very house itself felt hostility towards him and with each passing minute this feeling increased. Suddenly, from inside the pantry, he heard a strange rustling and shaking noise. He then saw to his amazement two hands appear over the top of the door and pull the dust sheet into the pantry!

'A moment later there was a whistle, low and eerie; the door opened wide, and I got a horrible shock as there came out my white dust sheet with a head lolling on top of it. For some seconds it remained silent and motionless, just outside the pantry door. Then it whistled again, the same low whistle.'

The handyman grabbed a hammer and shouted at the figure to stop trying to scare him, assuming he was being made the victim of a practical joke on the part of a member of the vicar's staff. The figure's response to his shouts was to dash past him and take up a new position near a staircase.

Rattlesden village. (Figgis-West)

'As it made this rush it dropped the sheet and I was horrified to see that it was naked – a thing with pale, blotchy skin of the colour of old parchment. For a few moments I watched this apparition in a state of benumbed perplexity, and as I watched it my brain seemed to begin to grow muzzy. I felt some force was passing from the thing in the corner to me: it seemed to be some foul influence which was thrusting itself upon my brain and sapping all the powers of my mind and body. I felt that my consciousness was gradually being smothered by a thick black mist. As I stood there half- dazed the thing began to move again – in a kind of crouching posture. I have said it was naked and shaped like a man. But I could not see its face distinctly – only a kind of phosphorescent glow. I wondered if the thing had eyes – I could not see them. Anyway, it appeared to be blind, for it came towards me with arms outstretched, just as a man would advance if he were feeling his way in the darkness. I had a sickening, overwhelming feeling of evil and was conscious once again of that sour, musty smell. It was an intense smell now and I was somehow certain that it was the smell of death.'*

The apparition grabbed the man and for an instant he could feel its face pressed close to his. He later described the skin as being like that of a wizened pig's bladder. What made this sight even more terrible was the dried-up blue-looking tongue which could be seen hanging from its mouth. As they struggled, the smell became even worse and he fainted. When he awoke, the foul creature had vanished but the smell remained. He fled the rectory, vowing never to return.

The man later discovered that others had also seen the ghost. The pantry door appeared to be the centre of activity and servants would often find the door held against them as if

St Nicholas Church, Rattlesden. (Figgis-West)

someone was holding it from the other side. The door was also known to open and close of its own accord. Indeed, it became so bad that one vicar had the door nailed up. This only seemed to make matters worse and he soon found the house plagued with bangs, thumps and the sound of iron pots and pans rattling from within the sealed pantry. Dogs also refused to stay in the house, becoming unnerved by some unseen presence before fleeing in terror.

It emerged that a certain Robert Bumpstead, a former inhabitant of the rectory, had died there in 1780. He had been heavily in debt and his creditors were hoping to seize his body and, one assumes, sell it to the medical profession who were always on the lookout for fresh corpses for the dissection table. The unfortunate man had been buried under the bricks of the pantry floor in order to thwart their plans and a tell-tale coffin-shaped depression was pointed out to the curious as the site of his final resting place.

In 1892 the old rectory was demolished and the skeleton of Bumpstead was unearthed and reburied in the churchyard. It appears that being interred in consecrated ground did little to calm his soul, and locals soon started to report that he now 'walked' the churchyard grounds. It was said that his spirit became so troublesome that the local clergy were finally forced to exorcise him using the traditional method of bell, book and candle. After this, his unhappy spirit was never seen again.

But perhaps the modern-day residents of Rattlesden should not rest too easily in their beds and assume that their sleepy village is now spook free. The village is home to another ghost. In 1815 a resident of the village, a Mr Atterwell, was caught stealing. Rather than face disgrace and punishment, he decided to hang himself. Suicides were denied Christian burial at the time and his body was taken to the riverside where a stake was driven through his heart in order to prevent his ghost returning to bother the living. He was then buried at the spot. Unfortunately, this method proved rather ineffective and his ghost is still said to haunt the river at midnight, splashing about and generally making a nuisance of himself.

CHAPTER THREE
BROTHER IGNATIUS

A vicarage can be found in the Fenland village of Elm which lies in Cambridgeshire not far from the Norfolk border. After World War Two, it was home to the Reverend Arnold Bradshaw, a former RAF chaplain, his wife Irene and their 19-year-old daughter, Suzette. The family had only been living in the property a short time when they became disturbed by unexplained footsteps which could be heard night after night in the upper parts of the house. Frequent searches by the reverend failed to provide an explanation. Mrs Bradshaw also heard a tolling bell coming from the attic. She noted that this always seemed to occur at 3am on the morning prior to a death in the parish. She later confirmed that she had heard the bell 31 times in just over two and a half years! No other family member heard the bell but her husband did confirm that his wife would mention hearing a bell tolling. He also added that news of a local death always followed this within a few hours.

Matters came to a head when Mrs Bradshaw witnessed a phantom monk in brown habit and sandals in an upstairs corridor. It vanished but, from that moment on, she would see it in various parts of the house. She felt no fear and often had a feeling of sadness when she saw him. She would say '*Bless You*' in order to make him feel welcome as she felt that he had as much right to be in the rectory as she and her family did. On one occasion, he told her '*Do be careful*' after she brushed against him in an upstairs corridor. She later explained that these words had not been spoken to her in the usual way but had come 'to her in her mind'. Mrs Bradshaw was apparently little troubled by the monk's admonishment and boldly asked who he was, '*Bless You. Can I help you? Can you tell me your name? You are very welcome here.*' The monk replied '*Ignatius, the bell-ringer*'. After this, the monk started to appear more frequently and, in conversations with Mrs Bradshaw, revealed that he had died some 700 years ago in a monastery which had stood on the site of the Georgian rectory. He said that for centuries he had been waiting for someone with whom he could communicate and added that she was the first woman he had ever spoken to.

Brother Ignatius.

The monk said that one of his responsibilities in life had been to watch the waters of the surrounding Fens and warn his brothers by tolling a bell if flooding threatened the monastery. One night he fell asleep and failed to ring the bell as the waters started to rise. The area was flooded and several of the monks drowned. Ignatius was disgraced and never got over the fact that his negligence had resulted in tragedy. In death, as a penance, he had continued to toll the bell every time someone had died in the parish.

Mrs Bradshaw described Ignatius as first appearing as a fine outline which slowly formed into a solid looking man of about 33 with 'dark curly hair and thin ascetic features'. He was described as always wearing a brown monk's habit which appeared old and very worn. The figure would appear, usually at dusk, and had been seen in the upstairs corridor, the parlour and at various other locations in the rectory.

Mrs Bradshaw clearly had mediumistic abilities and was not in the least bit concerned that she shared her home with a 700-year-old monk. Although Ignatius was not visible to the rest of the family, his presence was confirmed by the actions of the family terrier, Kik. Once, when Irene and her daughter were in the lounge, Ignatius entered and sat down on a vacant chair. The dog ran towards the monk and jumped onto his knees. The daughter pointed with shock at the terrier, which to her was now happily sitting in mid-air!

One September evening Mrs Bradshaw was preparing to go to sleep in a bedroom which was usually reserved for visitors to the rectory. She was accompanied by Kik but for some reason the dog appeared distressed and refused to settle. He ran out of the room three times before she could finally get him to stay with her.

Mrs Bradshaw then put out the light and soon fell asleep. At some point in the night she was disturbed abruptly by the feeling that something was being placed around her neck. She quickly grabbed a nearby torch and discovered to her relief that it was just a tendril of wisteria from outside the open bedroom window. It had somehow entered the room and had ended up laying across her throat. She started to pull it away when suddenly she became aware that the bedclothes were being pulled from her. She then found herself being picked up and thrown violently across the bed. Now terrified and wide awake, she became aware of a black, hazy shape which was moving towards her. A pair of hands suddenly appeared and made a grab for her throat. Unable to scream due to fear, she felt two rough and twisted hands gradually tightening around her throat. It seemed to her that death was now only seconds away.

It was at this point that another phantom appeared in the room. It was Ignatius. He moved towards the bed and grabbed the hands that were trying to squeeze the life out of her. Mrs Bradshaw was then able to free herself and fell back on the bed. The black form was still there, however, and it again moved towards her. She later described it as having a huge head and red face. Her dog attacked the thing and she took this opportunity to escape from the room and rush to her husband who was sleeping soundly in an adjoining bedroom. Peter Underwood investigated this case and interviewed the rector and his wife. Both confirmed that after the attack marks and bruises could be seen on her throat for several days. Underwood also spoke to a local doctor who confirmed that he too had seen the marks on her neck. The room was never used again after this attack and the door was always kept securely locked and bolted.

When she next saw the phantom monk she asked Ignatius if he knew who had attacked her. He replied that a previous occupant of the rectory had been murdered in that room and that it was the spirit of the murdered victim who had attacked her. He went on to explain that by saving her life he had gone some way to easing his conscience over the deaths of his brother monks and was now hopeful of forgiveness and final rest in the next life. After this, his appearances became less and less frequent, until he was seen no more.

Mrs Bradshaw was always convinced that she would have died that night but for the intervention of Ignatius. Today, the rectory of Elm is quiet and apparently untroubled by either the spirit of the monk or murdered man. It appears that Brother Ignatius has at last found peace and forgiveness after centuries of guilt and sorrow.

CHAPTER FOUR
YORK: BRITAIN'S MOST HAUNTED CITY

I have loved York ever since I was a child. Its history and its ghosts have always fascinated me. It is not surprising to learn that York is widely regarded as the most haunted city in Britain with the apparitions of Roman soldiers, cavaliers, Grey Ladies, and monks seemingly commonplace. Indeed, it has been calculated that the city can boast at least 140 ghosts!

Here are just some of the fascinating ghost stories to be found in this historic city.

YORK MINSTER

In 1964 work was being carried out on the West Front of York Minster. A team of stonemasons were busy replacing and repairing the weathered stonework as a lady stopped

The city walls of York.

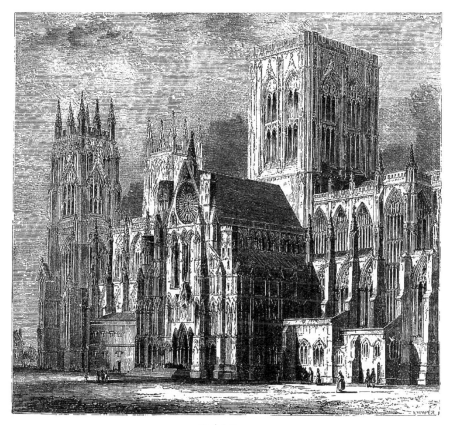

York Minster.

to watch them. She was particularly attracted to a fine piece of mediaeval carving. As she gazed at it, she was joined by a short man, scruffily dressed and wearing a cloth hat. He smiled and said, *'I carved that. Do you like it?'* As she turned to answer him, he faded away.

Thomas Gale was Dean of York in the late 17th century. He proved a popular man and was greatly mourned when he died in 1702. Six weeks after he died a Mr Hawley was asked to read a lesson at a service of Holy Communion in the Minster. He gave the reading in the pulpit but then appeared to become transfixed to the spot as if held by some unearthly force. A clergyman went up to him and tugged at his coat, whereupon Mr Hawley was released from his stupor and stumbled out of the pulpit. He was asked what was wrong and explained that as he had finished the reading he had looked in the direction of the choir and had been shocked to see Dean Gale sitting in his usual seat. The good dean still visits the Minster from time to time and has always been seen in the seat that he occupied in life.

In 1829 the Minster was the scene of an arson attack when a mentally ill man, Jonathan Martin, tried to burn down the building. He believed that he was acting on behalf of God and had hidden in the Minster after it had been closed to the public. He then sneaked out, stripped himself naked and started smashing up furniture in the choir before setting it alight. Fortunately, the fire was discovered by choristers arriving for morning service and the alarm was raised. The fire was finally brought under control but not before a large part of the building had been badly damaged. Martin was declared insane and committed to an asylum where he died in 1838. His naked ghost is said to haunt the Minster. The choir, the scene of his crime, is his favoured spot.

Following the fire, it was decided to hire night-watchmen to guard the building against further attack. In 1879 one of them, William Gladin, was sitting in the nave with his dog. Suddenly, the dog jumped up and ran into the north transept. Gladin followed it and saw a column of blue light, the height of a man, under the north-west tower. It suddenly moved to the middle of the great west door and then glided up the centre aisle towards the south transept. It then remained stationary for some ten minutes before flickering and vanishing from view through the wall. Gladin found his dog cowering by the door. Nothing could persuade the dog to enter the Minster again.

The Minster is also haunted by a man in Elizabethan clothing. He was seen walking down the nave in broad daylight by a school teacher and a group of children. The north transept is home to two female ghosts. They have been observed near a window dedicated to nurses who looked after soldiers during World War One.

A dog called Seamus was said to have been bricked up in a wall of the Minster centuries ago by a callous workman. His bark is still occasionally heard in the building after the crowds have left for the day.

Finally, a man once complained that his enjoyment of a concert had been spoilt by an inconsiderate monk who had been constantly walking up and down the aisle. He was rather surprised to learn that none of the other concert-goers or staff had seen the monk in question.

THE ROMAN BATHS

York is a Roman foundation and can boast some of the finest examples of Roman remains in the country, including fortress walls and part of the legionary headquarters which now lies beneath the Minster. The legionary bathhouse can be found in St Sampson's Square and was excavated in the late 1920s after work began on a new public house. The caldarium (hot room) and parts of the frigidarium (cold immersion bath) and tepidarium (warm room) are visible. The remains date from the fourth century, although there may have been an earlier set of baths on the site.

The Roman baths. (Figgis-West)

White spheres of light (orbs) have been captured on film and the sounds of footsteps and splashing have been heard. Some visitors have felt something invisible brush against them. In the early 1990s a former landlord and his friend decided to spend a night in the baths for charity. Both men saw a white light and the figure of a person. The apparition was seen to fade away in the area of the cold room. One of the men, the manager, saw a similar light a fortnight later. It was reflected in a mirror and faded as though being sucked into a hole. He decided to vacate the premises for good after this second experience!

A decorator employed to paint the bottom of the staircase that leads into the baths refused to continue with his work as he felt that 'something was there'.

In 2003 a medium, Diana Jarvis, was taken to the baths to see what she could discover. She sensed two men discussing politics and a woman giving birth who was attended by three women, including a priestess. The priestess was acting on behalf of a Hesta or Hestia and the child's name was Caldus. A smell like juniper berries and a 'fresher smell than pine' was also experienced by the medium. The latter, she felt, had an apparent drug-like effect.

Rachel Lacy, a York ghost hunter, had a vision of a Roman soldier and a slave during a séance. She also heard footsteps and heard a voice say *'save me'* as she stood in the caldarium.

Bizarrely, the ghost of an English Civil War soldier has also been seen in the baths.

THE NATIONAL RAILWAY MUSEUM

One of the sleeping cars is haunted by a former passenger. He has been seen looking out of the windows wearing an old-fashioned suit and rie. He is described as having 'something odd' about him.

The re-erected pedestrian railway bridge in the Great Hall fills some with a sense of panic when crossing it. It is claimed that a man once threw himself from the bridge into the path of an oncoming train. A ghostly woman has been seen walking through the hall and the sounds of whistling have also been heard.

The visitor's toilets are also the scene of psychic activity. The ladies' toilets are haunted by a man. A member of staff was washing her hands there when she made fun of the supposed ghost to a colleague. She suddenly had her hair pulled back by an invisible presence. Her friend saw her head jerk back as she screamed in shock.

The gift shop has been the scene of poltergeist disturbances. A security guard was patrolling the area and found a rack of postcards thrown to the floor. He had walked through the shop five minutes before and had found nothing out of place.

A travelling post office is the haunt of a former postal clerk who appears reluctant to give up his earthly work. In the mid-1980s, the wife and child of a member of staff visited the museum, but complained about a mannequin of a man in a grey suit sitting on a stool and smoking a pipe in the carriage. The child had found it 'a little scary'. The carriage in question had no mannequin on display.

The National Railway Museum. (Figgis-West)

Visitors have also captured strange figures and light anomalies on film. One photo of the Mallard shows a white figure standing by the train. Another photo was taken by a security guard in South Yard. It shows a man in old-looking clothing climbing aboard the cab of a train. It was taken on a night the museum was closed and empty of visitors. The figure was again seen in the early 1990s. During an exhibition in 2011, a hazy, blueish figure was captured on camera hovering next to some carriages.

In 2008 a figure was seen walking along one of the royal carriages during a ghost hunt. A member of staff confirmed that the apparition had been seen before on several occasions.

ST CRUX CHURCH

Elliott O'Donnell, the famous author of many books on the paranormal, was told of a policeman who was passing the mediaeval church one night. He was somewhat surprised to hear the Funeral March being played on the organ. He could see no funeral carriages outside but noticed that the music had begun to soften and finally stop. The door of the church suddenly opened and he could hear the sounds of rustling dresses. He could see nothing but could even feel the swish of the garments as they passed him. The doors then closed and all was quiet again.

The figure of a tall man was often seen looking intently into the street from a window inside the church. He was always observed in the early hours of the morning. He used to

St Crux Church.

appear so frequently that women on the way to work would shout out to him but he never showed any signs of being aware of their existence.

O'Donnell also wrote of a white-faced man seen peering into the church from one of the windows during daytime services. People even watched the church from outside at the same time as the figure was seen looking inside. Nothing was visible to them.

Another ghost mentioned by O'Donnell is that of a female figure in a shroud who would emerge from the graveyard and follow people to Fossgate where it vanished. At other times it would follow people down Collier Street and St Andrew Gate, vanishing as it reached Spen Lane.

St Crux's last ghost was a young woman in a white gown who used to follow the Waits of York, four or five men who were employed in winter to play music, act as watchmen, weather forecasters and give out the time. The figure would emerge from the churchyard and follow them until they reached Goodramgate where she would disappear. Attempts to communicate with her always proved unsuccessful. She would never respond to people who attempted to speak to her and would always vanish if approached. Whether or not she was the same phantom as O'Donnell's figure in the shroud is unclear.

St Crux was demolished in 1887 after being declared structurally unsafe. St Crux Parish Hall now stands on the site and was built using stones from the church.

MICKLEGATE BAR

Micklegate Bar is one of the mediaeval gateways into the city. Parts of it date back to the 12th century and the heads of executed traitors were displayed on the gate as a warning to any who contemplated plotting against the Crown. A feeling of terror and being watched have been experienced by some visitors as they pass beneath the Bar. Small glowing red lights have been reported swaying from left to right as people have looked up at the battlements. Some even claim to have felt warm liquid dropping on them from above.

Micklegate had a live-in gatekeeper and in 1797 this was Thomas Brocklebank. He lived there with his family, including Sara, his daughter. His job was to lock the gate each night as the curfew bell tolled and then reopen it at dawn the next day.

Sarah occasionally locked the gate when her father was busy elsewhere. On her birthday in 1797, she invited several friends to the gate for a party. That evening, as Thomas went to lock the gate, he was annoyed to discover that the keys had gone missing. He assumed that his daughter or one of her friends had hidden the keys for a joke and ordered her to find them.

Sarah was unable to do this and the gatekeeper and his family were thrown out for losing the keys. Thomas never spoke to his daughter again. The shock unhinged her mind

10390. - YORK MICKLEGATE BAR.

and she spent the rest of her life searching for the keys. Some 40 years later the Mayor of York was entertaining friends in his parlour when the door was thrown open and Sarah rushed in. She looked at the mayor and then declared, *'Have found them'* twice before falling dead. She was searched but the keys were nowhere to be seen.

The tragic ghost of Sarah is said to have returned to Micklegate Bar. Poltergeist activity has been reported in the building with lights switching on of their own accord and visitors touched by unseen hands. A shadowy figure has also been seen.

The smell of a wet dog has been noticed inside. This is believed to be connected with one of the last gatekeepers who lived here in the 19th century, who kept a long-haired dog.

John V. Mitchell, the author of a book on the ghosts of York, records talking to a lady who was visiting the city. She was walking along the walls to the Bar when she was seized by acute terror and an icy feeling around her solar plexus. She pressed herself against the wall and wondered how she could get off the defences. She then saw the lower half of a man wearing brown sandals. He wore a black gown and she even noticed the fine blond hairs of his legs. She then heard a male voice speak to her firmly, 'Don't be afraid. Follow me!' She followed the feet and after a short distance, they vanished. The feeling of terror then passed.

MARGARET CLITHEROW

The story of Margaret Clitherow is a tragic one. She was born in 1556, the daughter of Thomas Middleton, Sheriff of York. She married John Clitherow, a wealthy butcher and chamberlain of the city. She converted to the Catholic faith and fell foul of the law by refusing to attend church services. She then began to harbour priests, a capital offence under Elizabeth I. In 1586 she was arrested but refused to plead to prevent a trial and save her children from being questioned and possibly tortured. The punishment for refusing to plead was pressing to death. Margaret was denied food for several days and she was only allowed puddle water to drink. She was then taken to the Toll Booth at Ouse Bridge. Despite being pregnant, she was stripped naked and had a handkerchief tied across her face. She was laid across a sharp rock the size of a man's fist and the door from her own house was placed on top of her. Stones were then placed on the door to cause the rock beneath to break her back. She died within 15 minutes.

A house in the Shambles is now a shrine – Margaret was canonised by the Catholic church in 1970. Visitors to the house have often commented on the intense sense of peace and

Margaret Clitherow.

Jam hiems transiit, imber-
abiit, et recessit: surge, amica
mea, et voni: —Off. Parv.
B. Mariæ ad Vesperas.

calm within the building. Others have claimed to have felt Margaret's presence there. A man even claimed to have seen her one morning walking down the Shambles.

A hand, said to be hers, is kept in the Bar Convent in York

THE DAVYGATE TIME SLIP

The year was 1958 and two ladies were walking along the street when suddenly the buildings around them appeared to shimmer and vanish. Open fields now stood before them in which a battle was being fought between the Romans and Celts. The Romans were recognisable in full legionary armour while their Celtic opponents were seen to be more lightly dressed with spiky hair and body paint. The scene vanished after a few seconds. It has been surmised that the two women witnessed a battle dating from the Roman conquest of the north in the first century AD.

5 COLLEGE STREET

This stone building may seem innocuous but it hides a terrible past. In the 1930s a child's voice was heard to call out from one of the bedrooms. The parents would go up to check but found their children sleeping soundly. This happened on several occasions. The sounds of sobbing were heard by one of the children and the other child also claimed to have seen a young girl skipping about upstairs.

5 College Street.

A medium was contacted and they agreed to hold a seance in the house. The medium claimed to have made contact with a girl who was seven when she died. She said that the plague had come to the city in the 17th century. A member of her family had caught the disease and the house had been sealed by the authorities to prevent the infection from spreading to the neighbouring houses. Over the next few days, the sickness gradually killed the rest of the family until only the girl was left. Terrified, the girl went upstairs to a bedroom where she died of starvation.

Her sobbing is still heard from time to time and some have even claimed to have seen a child's face staring at them from the upper floor window.

A different account claims that the tragedy occurred during a plague in the middle ages. According to this version of events, the parents fled the house in a panic, leaving their daughter to die alone.

ST OLAVE'S CHURCH

This church dates from 1050 but was extensively rebuilt in the 15th century. It is dedicated to St Olaf, the patron saint of Norway.

Mrs Peggy Atkinson, a regular churchgoer here, once saw a lady and a boy in one of the pews at the front of the church. Both appeared to be dressed in old-fashioned looking

St Olave's Church, Mary-gate, York

clothes dating from the time of World War One. The boy was weeping and Mrs Atkinson noticed that the woman was hugging and comforting him. Mrs Atkinson then knelt in prayer and upon looking up noticed that the lady and the boy had suddenly vanished. She questioned the verger as to their identity. He denied having seen them, even though he was sitting in the same back pew as Mrs Atkinson. He insisted that no strangers had been present in the church that day.

THE KING'S MANOR

The King's Manor dates from the 15th century and was originally built to house the abbots of St Mary's Abbey. It later became the home of the governor of York, a school for the blind and is now leased to the University of York.

The house can boast several ghosts, including a Green Lady, so-called because she wears a 16th-century style green dress. She carries a bunch of roses in her hands and was seen in a wing added to the building in 1900. A maid scrubbing the floors one afternoon fainted after seeing the ghost emerge from a cupboard and walk right through her! The apparition appeared to be carrying a bunch of red ribbons in her hands. The maid claimed to have seen the apparition several times after this and always in the afternoon. It was only then that she realised the ribbons were, in fact, roses. The wife of a member of staff decided to watch for the ghost too but failed to see anything as the maid cried out, *'There she is. Can't you see her?'* However, she did hear rustling sounds as if someone was passing by her in a full-length dress. The maid finally returned to her home in Ireland and the Green Lady was never seen again. People were puzzled as to why a ghost from the Tudor period should appear in a new part of the manor. John V. Mitchell researched the case and found that the new wing actually stood on the site of a former rose garden.

Some claim the apparition to be Anne Boleyn, the second wife of Henry VIII. Anne – if the ghost is indeed her – did stay at the manor for a short period during her marriage to Henry, but why she should be drawn back to a place that she only visited once in her earthly life has not been explained.

The cowled figure of a monk dressed in black also wanders the corridors and a teacher used to hear a sound like the crack of a whip every night at 2.50am. This went on for several weeks. A cupboard door would also refuse to stay shut but only when a scarf of Royal Stuart tartan was placed there.

The north wing is supposedly haunted by Sir Henry Hastings, Earl of Huntingdon. Henry was the president of the Council of the North during the reign of Elizabeth I, a body originally established during the time of Edward IV to administer Royal justice in

The King's Manor.

the northern parts of England. King's Manor was his official residence as president and he carried out several improvements to the building, including constructing a new staircase which he now haunts.

One Halloween, before World War Two, four teachers decided to hold a vigil in one of the rooms in the manor. The room in question had two doorways – one led to the staff rooms and the other, used by the pupils, had a flight of stone steps which led down into the room itself. At midnight they all saw a figure descend the steps, wearing silk breeches, buckled shoes and a coat. Sadly, the appearance of the phantom was cut short by the sudden appearance of the headmaster who was less than impressed with the teacher's paranormal investigations and ordered them to their beds. It has been surmised that this apparition may have been Sir Henry Hastings who appears reluctant to leave his old home.

A painting of an unknown man in Stuart clothing hangs in a room off the staircase. In the 1930s and 1940s, it was often found lying on the floor undamaged. The hook on which it hung was still in place and it appeared that the portrait had been lifted off the wall by unseen hands.

The courtyard is haunted by the groans and screams of parliamentarian soldiers who were brought here after the battle of Marston Moor in 1644. A large number of them died due to their wounds or infection brought on by the unsanitary conditions in which they were kept.

THE THEATRE ROYAL

The Theatre Royal stands partly on the site of St Leonard's Hospital, supposedly the largest mediaeval hospital in the north of England – fragments of the hospital are still visible within the theatre. It was run by Augustinian nuns and monks who provided medical and spiritual care for the sick and infirm of York until Henry VIII's Dissolution of the Monasteries in the 1500s.

A legend states that a nun became pregnant here after having an affair with a York citizen and was punished for breaking her vows by being walled up alive – the site of which is reputed to be in the wall of a dressing room behind the dress circle. Her ghost, known as the Grey Lady, now haunts the theatre. The dressing room is reported to have a cold, uneasy feeling about it and actors often ask to be moved from there as they have sensed being watched by unseen eyes.

One actress, Marjorie Rowland, was once standing at the back of the dress circle when she saw the small figure of a nun, dressed in grey with a white coif, leaning over a stage box.

Another account tells of the Grey Lady appearing during the final rehearsal of a play, *Dear Octopus*, in 1974. One of the actors missed his lines and was seen by his fellow cast members to be staring intently into the dress circle. They turned to where he was looking and saw a glowing light. It gradually turned into the shape of a woman sitting in one of the seats. She looked down at them before vanishing. The production was a great success and the appearance of the Grey Lady before a new production was regarded from then on as a sign of success.

A seance was held in the theatre in the 1980s and it was claimed that the nun, who was supposedly called Therese, had been contacted. She denied having an affair and said she had been guilty of falsely claiming to have seen angels during mass. She was punished by being locked in a room with a warning that she would remain there, or be

The Theatre Royal. (Figgis-West)

punished even more harshly, if she continued to tell lies, as none of the other nuns present during the mass had witnessed the angelic beings. Following these messages a ceremony was held with a priest which allowed the nun to move on to the next world.

The theatre also houses another ghost, an actor from the 1770s or 1780s. He fancied himself as a ladies' man and was always very well-dressed and wore a large emerald ring on one of his fingers. He soon turned his amorous attentions to one of the chorus girls. The lady was already spoken for and her boyfriend naturally objected to his rival's attempts to seduce her. The two quarrelled in nearby Blake Street with the result that the actor was stabbed to death. The actor had been due to appear on stage that very night and it was decided to use his understudy instead. It is claimed that as the curtain was raised the ghost of the murdered man appeared on stage. The rest of the cast were naturally shocked, especially when the apparition promptly vanished!

The actor's ghost was often seen in the theatre after that, always smartly dressed with a fine emerald ring on his finger. His last appearance was in the 1960s.

Finally, the theatre was briefly haunted in the 1930s by organ music. The sound of playing was heard at 2.20am one morning and then again exactly an hour later. There had never been an organ in the building and the origin of the sounds heard that night still remain a mystery.

ALL SAINTS, NORTH STREET

It was Christmas Eve 1953 and Tony Walker had arranged to meet his mother and some friends at the mediaeval church of All Saints following a midnight mass. As he waited, he noticed a family friend sitting in a small garden nearby. She came over to the railings and, using a nickname only known to him, said hello and wished him a Merry Christmas. Mr Walker had to cut short his conversation with her as his friends were now leaving the church, and when they turned into North Street he mentioned to his mother that he had just seen their friend in the garden.

All Saints. (Figgis-West)

Later, in January, Mr Walker was shocked to learn that the lady in question had died in the November of the previous year – a month before he had seen and spoken to her in York!

YORK CASTLE MUSEUM

The Castle Museum, housed in the city's 18th-century prison, is one of York's most popular attractions, with its reconstructed Victorian street and Dick Turpin's cell just two of the many highlights that bring visitors here each year from across the globe. As a child I can remember visiting the museum and being particularly fascinated by a Victorian model of an execution. You put a coin in the slot, heard a tolling bell, and then witnessed a tiny figure being hanged for some undisclosed crime. Such were the entertainments provided here for children in the 1970s!

The museum can also boast a few ghost stories.

Members of a TV crew were filming in the Victorian street when they were disturbed by the sounds of a woman singing. It was assumed that the singing formed part of the sound effects used by the museum to enhance the visitors' experience. A staff member climbed the stairs to the room where the sound equipment was held and as he opened the door the singing stopped. A check of the equipment showed that it was turned off and so could not be responsible for the singing they had all heard.

Singing was also heard in the condemned cell when the heath and safety manager stayed there overnight as part of a charity fund-raising event. It is hardly surprising that he bid a hasty retreat to the museum offices above after hearing the sounds.

York Castle Museum. (Figgis-West)

Apparitions have been seen in the museum too. A lady in Victorian clothing was once witnessed by a tour guide and a boy in 1930s or 1940s attire has been spotted in the Military Gallery. A small dog haunts the museum and a visiting teacher once saw an elderly woman sitting in front of a fireplace. She told one of the guides and the pair returned to the room in question. The woman had vanished.

Strange shadows linger near the site of the gallows and the sounds of rattling chains, screams and a slamming cell door also break the stillness of the air in the cells and half-moon court. Another guide once heard the sounds of scratching coming from the corner of a cell floor. An examination of the floor revealed the word 'innocent' scratched into the flagstones.

In 2012 John Burnside and his family from Wakefield were visiting the museum and took several photos in the cells. Some were later found to contain the image of a girl in a Victorian dress. Mr Burnside was adamant that no one resembling the figure had been seen by him when taking the pictures. He also insisted that the photos had not been tampered with.

CHAPTER FIVE
THE SPECTRES OF EDINBURGH CASTLE

Edinburgh Castle is regarded as one of Scotland's finest monuments and is home to the Stone of Scone, the National Scottish War Memorial and the Scottish Regalia. The castle has dominated the city for centuries and can bear witness to many tales of sieges, torture, witch burnings and executions. With such a history, it is hardly surprising to learn that the castle is reputed to be one of the most haunted places in Scotland.

THE PIPER

During building work at the castle centuries ago (some sources claim the story actually dates from the early 19th century) workmen came across the entrance to a tunnel that appeared to lead south in the direction of Holyrood Palace. To discover how long it was, a young piper was sent in with orders to play his bagpipes so that his progress could be followed from above. The piper's muffled playing could be heard as he travelled under the road and a group followed the sounds until they suddenly stopped. No attempt was made to discover what had happened to the unfortunate piper and the entrance was quickly sealed up.

It is said that the sounds of bagpipes can occasionally still be heard wafting up through the Royal Mile.

THE DRUMMER

In 1650 the castle's governor was one Colonel Walter Dundas. One night a guard on duty heard the sound of a drum being played. He noticed a figure walking along the battlements, beating out a warning of an impending attack. The guard called out a challenge but received no reply. He fired his musket at the figure and raised the alarm. Colleagues immediately rushed to his aid but a search of the castle grounds failed to locate the mysterious drummer. Others, including the governor, also saw and heard the drummer on subsequent nights.

These were troubled times for Scotland as their decision to support Charles II following the execution of his father had resulted in Oliver Cromwell's New Model Army crossing the border to crush the uprising. It was suggested that the phantom drummer was sent as a warning of impending attack as Cromwell's forces later that year laid siege to the castle following the defeat of the Royalist army at Dunbar. The governor finally surrendered the castle in order to prevent further bloodshed.

The drummer has occasionally been seen and heard since the 17th century with some even claiming that the figure is headless. His last reported sighting was in 1960.

THE PHANTOM DOG

The castle has a soldier's pet cemetery. Visitors have claimed to have seen a dog running through the area. A search for the dog always proves fruitless.

CRISIS APPARITION

The year was 1689 and William of Orange had taken the throne after James II had fled England.

The Earl of Balcarres, a supporter of James, was a prisoner in the castle when from his bed he became aware of the presence of his friend, Viscount Dundee. After looking sadly at the earl, the figure left the chamber without a word. Balcarres, in great surprise, not suspecting that what he saw was a ghost, called out to his friend to stop but received no answer. He subsequently learned that at the very moment when the apparition stood before him, Dundee had fallen at the Battle of Killiecrankie.

THE TUNIC

The castle restaurant was the scene of some activity in 2001 when members of staff claimed to have seen a 19th century Royal Engineer's tunic moving behind a sealed glass case. During one function, the arm was seen to move on three occasions as if beating an invisible drum. The *Edinburgh Evening News* got hold of the story but the restaurant owners refused to comment. However, the paper did learn that one staff member had left their job in fear and returned home to France. One member of staff confirmed that they had all been terrified by what they had seen and was quoted as saying, *'There is a strange feeling in the restaurant and I blame the tunic.'*

THE SHADOW GHOST

In the 1920s a Colonel Street and his wife took up residence in a house in the castle precincts. They soon became aware of what they called 'the shadow ghost' which seemed to linger on the stairs and was described as 'a shadow the height of a human being'. Over

Edinburgh Castle.

time it began to become more solid and was also seen in a room at the top of the stairs. The figure would sometimes not be seen for ten days but would then suddenly reappear in the same spot as before. The figure also appeared to be aware of its surroundings as once it was seen to bend as if looking at a dustpan and brush left by a maid on the stairs.

Phantom cats also haunted the property. Mrs Street wrote to a friend called Caddell of what she had seen: *'They were never full face, always passing or back view, usually slinking downstairs ... they were not transparent. I saw them by day and by gaslight. They kept close to corners of the bannisters just as real cats would. The tails were certainly not up. They took no notice of me at all, no one else saw them except the one time my husband saw one.'* The cats she saw were described as dark but the one seen by her husband was grey. Mrs Street also saw what she described as smaller 'things' on the ceiling.

An 'occultist' called Mr Taylor was called in to rid the property of the phantoms and he apparently succeeded as Mrs Street confirmed that the 'shadow ghost' and cats were never seen again. A letter about the haunting was sent in 1926 to the *Society for Psychical Research* after the couple had left the castle.

PSYCHIC EXPERIMENTS

In April 2001 one of the largest paranormal experiments was conducted in Edinburgh. As part of the Edinburgh International Science Festival, Dr Richard Wiseman, a psychologist from Hertfordshire University, brought 250 volunteers to explore the castle and two other sites in Edinburgh as part of a ten-day investigation. Only those who knew nothing of Edinburgh's ghosts were allowed to take part after a careful screening process. It was also ensured that none of the volunteers were told which locations were supposedly haunted. Locations without any record of paranormal activity were also chosen as red herrings.

The team was broken up into groups and sent into the vaults below the castle that had once been used to incarcerate French and American prisoners during the Seven Years War, the American War of Independence and the Napoleonic Wars. By the end of the experiment half of those taking part reported experiences that they couldn't explain at the locations chosen. These included:

Feeling something tugging at clothes.
Something touching the face.
Seeing shadowy figures.
A sense of being watched.
A burning sensation on the arm.
Sudden drops in temperature.

Wiseman commented at the end of the experiment that the results were *'more extreme than expected'*. He also noted that most of the volunteer's experiences took place in the very locations reputed to be haunted but did not rule out that damp, lighting and room temperature could play a part in what they were feeling. Wiseman concluded that *'Whatever the explanation, it means there is something going on because otherwise, we would expect the distribution to have been more random.'*

OTHER HAUNTINGS

Other alleged ghosts in the castle include a prisoner who tried to escape in a dung cart but was discovered and killed, a coach pulled by black horses that leaves the castle gate and trundles along the Royal Mile and, finally, the phantom of Lady Janet Douglas of Glamis, who was accused of witchcraft and plotting to kill King James V. Her servants were tortured into falsely confirming her guilt, and in 1537 she was burnt at the stake in front of the castle. Her young son was forced to watch. Her ghost is said to roam the castle, weeping, Unexplained knocks are said to be a replay of the sounds of workman erecting the platform on which she was burnt.

CHAPTER SIX
WELSH PHANTOMS

THE DEATH CANDLE

Elliot O'Donnell spoke of a haunted house near the sea-front in Aberystwyth. A woman was staying with her aunt one Christmas and was sleeping in her aunt's room. She suddenly woke up and heard the clock on the landing striking one. She then noticed that the entire room was illuminated by a candle on the chimney-piece. It seemed to be burning with a greyish-blue light rather than the normal yellowish light. She assumed that her aunt had forgotten to put the candle out and got out of bed to blow it out. She returned to her bed only to realise that the candle was burning again!

She again left her bed and extinguished it. She waited to make sure it was out and then returned to her bed. You can imagine her alarm when the candle suddenly burst into life again!

It is hardly surprising that she hid in fear under the bedclothes and remained like that until morning. She thought of telling her aunt but decided against it as she was strict and would, no doubt, dismiss the story as simple fantasy or even a bad dream. She decided to tell Susan, the elderly maid, who had been with the family for years and would, she hoped, be more understanding.

The maid immediately went pale upon being told what had happened and said she was certain that it was an omen of the aunt's impending death. She explained that to see 'y canwyll corff' (the corpse candle) meant that someone was destined to die in the house. The maid had seen such a candle in the house the night before the death of the aunt's sister. The aunt had also told Susan that she had seen the corpse candle before the death of her own mother. The aunt had explained to the maid that the candle was 'a family haunting'.

The woman told O'Donnell that she tried to ease the fear of the maid by saying it was mere superstition. Sadly, Susan was proved correct in her prediction as the aunt died shortly after.

THE HAUNTED CAVE

Green Bridge Cave near Pendine is haunted by a fiddler who sheltered in the cave but lost his way and was never seen again. The faint sounds of him playing the fiddle have been heard by those who visit the area. Peter Underwood was told of a man in 1978 who, as a boy, had been playing near the cave with a friend. They both heard the sounds of faint music coming from the cave. They ran and told their parents but when they returned the music had stopped. Years later, the man and his wife were walking by the cave one evening when they both heard the sounds of a fiddle coming from inside. At first they dismissed it as a trick of the wind but then realised that the music had formed a tune. The couple entered the cave and the music became louder but then suddenly faded away. The man wanted to explore further and find the source of the music but his wife became fearful and persuaded him to give up the idea.

Some believe that the ghostly fiddler is trying to lead people to his final resting place so that he can receive a proper burial. Others believe that he is trying to lure others to their deaths so that they can join him in his lonely and endless wanderings beneath the earth.

THE WHITE HORSE OF OXWICH CHURCHYARD

In 1877 the Reverend J. D. Davies published a book, *A History of West Gower*, in which he described a very strange ghost that was said to haunt Oxwich churchyard at midnight:

My elder brother, now deceased, when a lad of about thirteen or fourteen years of age, had been out one evening with my father, fishing in the bay, it was late when they landed, and by the time they had finished mooring the boat it was nearly twelve o'clock.

Oxwich Churchyard. (Figgis-West)

They had just gained the top of the beach, where the path narrows leading the church, when my brother, happening to look behind him, saw what he described to me as a white horse walking on its hind legs and proceeding leisurely along the path towards the church gate.

Having called my father's attention to this strange spectacle, he turned round, and they both stood for a minute, and watched the creature or whatever it was, until it reached the gate, or rather the stone stile by its side, which the animal crossed apparently without the slightest difficulty, still going on its hind legs. The uncanny thing then disappeared.

The only remark my father made was 'Come along.' They were soon inside the rectory, which was only a few yards off.

This strange adventure was rarely afterwards spoken of by my father nor alluded to in any way. I have often been on the point of questioning him about it but some vague feeling of undefined alarm always prevented me. Both eye-witnesses have since passed away, so nothing further can be learnt on the subject.

THE HUMMING GHOST OF WYLFA NUCLEAR POWER STATION

Construction of the Wylfa Nuclear Power Station on Anglesey, now decommissioned, began in 1963. In August 1964 several Irish workmen were working on a sea tunnel during a night shift. They reported seeing a woman in white. Not long after, six men working in the same tunnel saw a woman in an evening gown standing near the edge of a cliff. She was humming a tune. Other workers also saw her and thought she was preparing for a swim in the sea. They called out to her but she ignored them and walked to the edge of the cliff and faded away.

Another man was having a tea break at 3am by a new road on the site. He reported seeing a woman dressed in a long white dress drift past the window of the building where he was sitting.

Many of the workmen became so unnerved by the ghost that they downed tools and refused to carry on working at the site.

It is thought that the ghost was Rosina Buckman, a New Zealand opera singer who found fame in England in the early decades of the last century. Later in life, when teaching at the Royal Academy of Music in London, she bought a country house, Galan Ddu on Wylfa Head. Rosina often brought students from the Royal Academy and they would give charity concerts in Cemaes Village Hall.

Rosina was described at this time as wearing long flowing white gowns and carrying a Pekinese dog under one arm. Rosina's mother-in-law Emma d'Oisley also loved the place and spent many happy days there with her daughter-in-law. Emma died in the house in 1935 and her ashes were buried in the grounds at her request.

During World War Two the Royal Air Force decided to build a radio location station on Wylfa Head and Rosina reluctantly had to sell the house.

When Wylfa Head was chosen as the site for a nuclear power station, the casket containing the ashes of Emma were removed and re-interred at Llanbadrig Church, Cemaes. It is surmised that the disturbance of her mother-in-law's ashes caused the haunting. It is said that Rosina still haunts the site of her former home and the surrounding area. The months of July and August are her most active time for those inclined to seek her out.

Rosina Buckman.

THE MAN IN GOLD

An ancient burial mound known as the Hill of the Goblins (Bryn-yr-Ellyllon) was long reputed to be haunted by a man all dressed in gold. The nearby road was also said to be the haunt of a headless warrior riding a grey horse which people assumed was the same phantom.

Around 1810 a woman and her drunken husband were crossing the field known as Cae'r Yspryd (Field of the Ghost) when they encountered the phantom. It was described as 'of unusual size, and clothed in a coat of gold, which shone like the sun.' It crossed before her, stopped momentarily on the burial mound, and then disappeared. It was said that the woman was scared 'into fits and the man into sobriety'. In 1828 a dressmaker also saw the ghost. She was so shocked upon seeing it that it sent her mad.

Another appearance of the ghost dates from 1819 and concerns a woman called Nancy who was herding her cows down the lane in the moonlight when she saw a golden man cross the track in front of her as it walked down Goblin's Hill.

Yet another sighting occurred one summer evening in 1830. A woman was riding home from the marketplace at nearby Mold. As she approached the mound, she noticed that

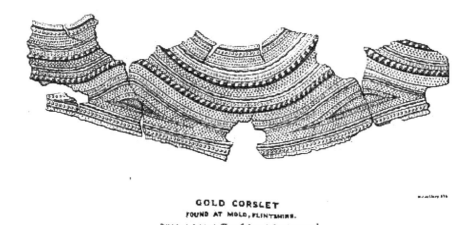

GOLD CORSLET
FOUND AT MOLD, FLINTSHIRE.
[Width of Original, Three feet one inch and a quarter]

The golden cape.

some of the trees on the opposite side of the road were illuminated by a strange light. She then saw a tall apparition clothed in golden armour. The figure emerged from the wood, crossed the road, and vanished into the mound. The woman was so shocked that she returned to Mold where she told her story to the vicar, C.B. Clough. He wrote an account of what she had seen and got 'three other respectable persons' to witness it.

The mound was levelled in 1833 and the skeleton of a tall man was found. A gold cape, dating to around 1900 BC, was found on top of him. It is surmised that the cape was used for ceremonial purposes and would have been worn by a person of very high status.

The stories of the ghostly man in gold all pre-date the discovery of the golden cape. It is hardly surprising to learn that believers in the supernatural have often cited this case as proving the reality of ghosts. Others, however, have suggested that the golden burial was preserved as a folk memory and passed on from generation to generation. If true, it is remarkable to think that the distant remembrance of a burial was kept alive for almost 4,000 years in the form of a ghost story.

The golden cape – now known as the Mold cape – is now displayed in the British Museum.

THE WOMAN IN WHITE

Oystermouth Castle is a ruined Norman castle that overlooks Swansea Bay. The ruin is also home to a ghostly White Lady with a bloody back.

A couple were cuddling beneath a tree one evening when they heard someone crying behind them. They got up and looked but could see no one. They then spotted a woman

Oystermouth Castle.

dressed in white, her head in her hands, vanish behind a tree. They searched the area but could find no trace of her.

A family were picnicking at the castle. The two children ran off to play but came back, very upset, to tell their parents of a woman crying behind a tree. Their father returned with them and saw a woman in a long white robe with a cord tied around her waist. She appeared to be crying but he could hear no sound. She then turned and he was shocked to see that her back was bleeding from a large number of cuts and wounds. He took the children to his wife and returned to the spot where he had first seen her. She had vanished.

A man was taking his dog for a walk near the castle ruins. The dog ran off and his repeated whistles failed to bring it back to him. He then saw the animal sitting by a tree, whimpering in fear. It was looking at part of the castle wall. It was getting dark but the man was keen to find out what had scared his dog. He moved forward and the dog suddenly started to howl. He then saw a white shape on the ground before him. As he got closer, he saw that it was a woman dressed in white. She rose and then appeared to vanish into the wall. He searched the area where he had last seen her but could find no entrance – the wall was solid stone.

Peter Underwood was told by a mother that her ten-year-old son had come running back to her one day saying that he had seen a lady with blood on her back crying near the castle. The mother returned with her son but could find no one.

A legend states that during the mediaeval period a woman was whipped to death in the dungeon for some unrecorded transgression. It is claimed that if you walk around the whipping post twelve times and then place a pin in the nail-marks, her phantom will appear at a nearby window. You have been warned!

THE GHOSTLY SAVIOUR

Our last ghost story in this chapter dates from the 19ᵗʰ century and concerns the Reverend John Jones, a minister at Bala, It was a hot summer's day and he was making for Machynlleth where he was due to hold a religious meeting. He paused at Llanuwchllyn to take a break and refreshment at a local inn. After drinking some ale he watered his horse and checked his large and expensive watch before moving on. It was at this point that he noticed a rough-looking man resting by a tree. A sickle, sheathed in straw, lay on the ground beside him. The man was looking at him intently but he thought no more of it and rode off.

The minister had been riding for over an hour when he noticed a man walking towards him and realised that it was the same man he had seen at the inn. Jones wondered to himself how he had got ahead of him without noticing. The man touched his hat in greeting and asked for the time. He then thanked the minister and wished him a good day. Jones rode on. The track went downhill and was bordered on both sides by a high hedge. At the end was a gate which led into a field. The minister rode on and noticed something was following him on the left-hand side of the hedge. At first he thought it was an animal but then realised it was the man who had asked for the time. He was now bent low and was carrying his sickle on his shoulder. Jones slowed down and saw that the man had stopped and was unsheathing the sickle. The minister realised to his horror that the man meant to attack and rob him. This feeling was confirmed when the man, doubled-up, ran towards the gate where he crouched in wait behind a bush.

Although Jones was only in his 30s, he was unarmed and would find it hard to defend himself against a man armed with a sickle. He looked around in the hope that someone else may be on the road, but he was alone. He thought of riding back but changed his mind after thinking of the people who had gathered to hear him preach. He would not be a coward and let them down. He considered riding hard for the five-barred gate and jumping over it but was worried that his ageing horse would fail to clear it. He then looked for a way through the hedge but the gaps were too narrow for his horse to pass through. He finally decided to pray for help. *I am a weak and sinful man, O Lord. Please show me what I must do.'* The prayer fortified him and he slowly rode on towards the gate. The horse suddenly shuddered as a man on a white horse rode by. He was dressed in black and appeared – to quote Jones – 'as if he had sprung out of the ground.' The minister surmised that he must have been riding behind him and had only caught up with him because he had stopped. He rode up to the stranger and asked if he had noticed the man with the sickle. The man did not reply. Jones then told him that he was hiding behind a bush and had probably planned to rob him of his watch after seeing it at the inn. The man still did not reply and rode on. The minister then asked if he could travel with him a short way as it was unlikely that the robber would attempt to attack them both. The man in black continued to ignore him and just stared straight ahead.

As they neared the gate the man with the sickle emerged from his hiding place and ran away. *'There he goes!'* Jones called out. *'You see, I did not imagine it. He saw there were two of us and thought better of his plan.'* This time the stranger nodded in agreement. They reached the gate and Jones dismounted. He pointed to the would-be robber running away over the brow of a hill. '*Can it be doubted for a moment that my prayer was heard and that you were sent by the Lord?'*

The minister then realised that he had only addressed the stranger in English and so repeated his last words in Welsh as he surmised that the man was a Welsh speaker. As he did so, the man turned to him and said, *'Amen.'* The minister then started to open the gate. When he turned back, the man had vanished into thin air.

CHAPTER SEVEN
THE KERSEY ENIGMA

Kersey in Suffolk has long been regarded as one of the most beautiful villages in all of England. It has been featured in film and TV and is often visited by tourists in search of the picturesque. The village was also once the location for a bizarre incident involving three teenagers.

One Sunday morning in October 1957, three 15-year-old Royal Navy cadets, William Laing, Michael Crowley and Ray Baker, were on a training exercise in rural Suffolk. They were based at HMS *Ganges* in Shotley and had been ordered to find the village of Kersey and then report back all they had seen within five hours. Crowley later recalled:

'Our class (no.262) was scheduled to go on a short weekend expedition. We were not informed where we were actually going. The class (20) left Ganges early Saturday afternoon and travelled for about 2 to 3 hours towards Ipswich and then through country roads and lanes. We eventually arrived at a farmyard and were billeted in a barn. The evening and night consisted of the usual meal and get-together.

The night had been cold and on the Sunday morning the sun was shining and there had been a frost, a very crisp sunny morning. When breakfast was over and the barn had been cleaned up we were assembled and then split into groups, our group consisting of three... the time would have been about 9am when we set off as it was still quite cold. As I remember we followed a road for a while and then cut across some fields.'

It was at this point that William Laing caught a hare in the bushes. It had flopped down in the long grass and appeared strangely unconcerned by its capture. The three decided to release it. They crossed more fields and came across a greyish stone cottage surrounded by trees. A farm worker with his wife and family were seen standing by the wall and gate. The boys asked them the way to Kersey. The farmer looked at them suspiciously but pointed and said, '*Hold in that direction.*'

Ten minutes passed and they found themselves approaching the village from the south east. It was around 12 noon. The church bells were ringing but as they climbed an iron fence, some 100 yards from the church, the bells suddenly stopped.

They entered a lane which led into the southern part of the village. It had a brown, dusty earthen surface with ancient-looking houses on one side. Part of the lane was lined with forest trees, tinged with a greenish light. The lane lead to a stream. Beyond this stood more old looking houses. The village appeared deserted and even the ducks stood silent and motionless beside the shallow stream – one of the boys likened them to decoys. The ducks showed no awareness of the three boys. There was no wind and even the birds in the trees remained silent. A small wooden bridge, consisting of four posts, two wooden planks and a handrail, crossed the stream and it was here that the boys stopped for 10 minutes. It was so hot that they removed their jerseys and drank from the stream. The church was not visible from where they squatted.

The boys were struck by the fact that although it was autumn, the trees in the village appeared fresh and green as they would in spring or early summer. Indeed, they stood in stark contrast to the ones they had seen outside the village which had displayed the usual autumnal colours associated with that time of year. The sky was intensely blue and the trees appeared unnaturally still. The area was also strangely devoid of shadows.

A wave of depression set in as the boys continued to sit by the stream. They noticed that none of the houses had TV aerials or telephone wires. Not even a parked car could be seen. They decided to move on. A butcher's shop was visible on the right-hand side of the lane, just beyond the stream. The door was painted green and two small windows were visible. The boys looked into one of the windows and saw that the inside was deserted and covered in cobwebs. Two or three skinned oxen carcasses, turned green and mouldy with age, were the only things visible within. The colour of the meat was described as 'almost an iridescent green' but the boys did not notice any smell originating from the carcasses. One of the boys commented on the waste of allowing such meat to rot. It appeared as if the place had been deserted for weeks. The boys then looked into another house and saw a deserted room, a staircase and whitewashed walls. Other houses were examined but the small, dull, greenish glass window panes made viewing inside impossible. None of the houses had curtains, window boxes or even gardens at the front. One building had a stone carving like a gargoyle above the door. The village appeared abandoned. There was no sign of a pub or shops.

The sense of unease continued. Sadness, unfriendliness and even a feeling of evil pervaded the air. Unseen beings appeared to watching the three and they took to their heels. The lane narrowed and the houses appeared closer together as they hurried on. As they left the lane the sound of the bells could be heard again and the smoke from village chimneys was seen rising in the air. It should be noted at this point that none of the boys

Kersey. (John West)

had seen smoke when in the village itself. Laing thought that they had been in the village for about 25 or 30 minutes.

They left the lane and entered the fields to the west of the village where they continued running to shake off the feeling of depression. They finally reported back to the petty officer in charge but he remained sceptical about their experiences and laughed off the hare incident. He did agree though that they had seen Kersey.

The story first came to light when Andrew Mackenzie, a paranormal researcher and Vice President of the Society for Psychical Research, put out an appeal for material in his 1982 book *Hauntings and Apparitions*. William Laing, now a retired Royal Navy wireless operator living in Australia, replied with his account of his experiences in Kersey. There was a series of correspondence between the two and Mackenzie sent Laing postcards of the village. Laing marked one with a cross. This indicated the possible butcher's shop. Mackenzie visited the house in question and discovered that a butcher's shop (now called Bridge House and dating back to 1350) had indeed stood where the boys had seen it. Records showed that the business dated back at least to the 1790s. It had closed in 1905 and had been turned into a shop and then into a private house. He was unable to establish if it had been a butcher's shop before 1790.

In September 1990 Laing revisited Kersey for the first time since 1957. He looked around the village with Mackenzie, Dr Hugh Pincott (former Hon. Secretary of the SPR) and Leslie Cockayne, a local historian and a member of an old Kersey family.

Laing noticed various changes to the village, including a number of houses where the boys had originally seen trees. None of the houses were new and all dated prior to the youth's 1957 experiences. He also noted that more houses now lined the other side of the lane. Again, these clearly dated to long before 1957. The window panes were now also much bigger than the ones he had seen before. The stream was now concrete based and ran in a different direction. The small bridge was also in a different position. Laing was surprised to see two pubs and asked, *'How could we have missed them?'* Both pubs dated back several hundred years. Laing also recalled that in 1957 the upper part of the lane had appeared narrower with overhanging buildings. Now it was wider – it was thought that the removal of some of these overhangs could have made the lane appear wider. A bare patch of greenery in a break of a row of houses puzzled Laing and Cockayne informed him that a house had stood there but had been knocked down about 80 or 90 years before. Paving stones, about 18 inches square, standing in the top of the lane had also vanished. The church was also clearly visible from the stream. The large trees surrounding the church had vanished.

Mackenzie also wrote to the two other witnesses, Michael Crowley and Ray Baker, to ask them for their account of that day in 1957.

Crowley agreed that they had seen 'something unusual'. Kersey reminded him of a Cotswold village and the one thing that really stood out in his mind was the rotting meat in the butcher's shop. Crowley remembered the three discussing the total absence of people with the suggestion being made that they were attending a church service. Crowley even wondered if the village had been evacuated during World War Two and never reoccupied. He was also surprised that the empty buildings had not been vandalised. Crowley also noted the absence of noise, cars, animals, church, pub, street lights, wires, and aerials. He remembered the street not being overgrown. He did disagree with Laing on one point. He remembered them encountering the hare after leaving the village.

Roy Baker could provide little. He remembered almost nothing of Kersey and had not noticed anything unusual during his time there.

So what had occurred on that autumn day in 1957?

Mackenzie concluded that the boys had found themselves in another era. The abandoned village and mediaeval appearance suggested to him a time when the Black Death (1348–39) had devastated Britain. Whole villages had been wiped out and research showed that Kersey had also been hit by the plague. He also noted that the church, including the tower, had been left unfinished at the time. Could this explain why the church had not been visible to the boys? Laing had said trees were growing on the hill where the church stood. These could have easily hidden a half-completed building. So had the three youths been transported back in time to the late 1300s? Or was their experience from the 1420s when the village was prospering again and the residents could afford window glass and recommencement of work on the church? Mackenzie favoured a date between 1420 and 1460 – although this latter date would not explain the abandoned butcher's shop or the seemingly abandoned houses.

Sceptics were soon to cast doubt on the whole story. It emerged that Kersey was not hooked up to mains electric until the early 1950s. This, they said, would explain the lack of wires and TV aerials. It was also pointed out that many of the buildings in the village are mediaeval and do not look very different from their original appearance. Three boys, all unfamiliar with the area, could have easily become confused with their surroundings and imagined themselves in an earlier time. Ray Barker had not noticed anything strange because there was nothing strange to see. And maybe the population had indeed been attending a church service at the time of the boy's visit.

However, the sceptics, as they often do, also chose to ignore those facts which did not fit in with their theories. The village had been wired to the mains electric in 1950 and telephone wires were visible in the village from at least the 1940s. And how could the boys look into a butcher's shop that no longer existed? Why had the meat been left to rot? Why were the houses empty? Why were the ducks motionless and seemingly oblivious to their presence? Why did the birds in the trees remain silent? Why were the trees in the village still green with summer foliage? Why did the boys see a dirt track when it was shown that it had been surfaced with pea shingle and tar several years before their visit? Why was the church tower not visible from the stream? And how do we explain the disappearance of the forest trees adjoining the lane, the lack of any wind or shadows and the absence of houses that were actually there before the boy's visit and so should have been visible to all three? And finally, what of the feeling of evil, hostility and of being watched?

Ray Baker was a cockney and was unused to being in a country village. This could explain why he failed to notice anything strange, although William did comment that Ray *had* been surprised at the time by the empty buildings during their visit to the village. And let us not forget that Baker had confirmed that he could remember very little of his time in Kersey.

William Laing was a Highlander and had always lived close to nature. He had been a poacher as a boy and was keenly aware of country sounds and even the change of light at different times of the year. He had been struck by the absence of bird song in the village and commented that he had never before or since experienced 'a still quiet such as at Kersey'. The strangeness of the place had stuck with him ever since that day in 1957. That a person used to the countryside should have felt so uneasy in Kersey is noteworthy.

Michael Crowley was also a country boy from Wiltshire and confirmed most of what Laing had said. He only disagreed with the timing of the hare incident.

Clearly, something had happened that day. The changed appearance of the village, the strange atmosphere, the lack of sounds and shadows and the feeling of being watched all point to something more than just unfamiliarity with the area.

So had the three youths briefly travelled back in time to mediaeval England? Some have suggested that the glass in the windows suggests a later time as glass was not common in houses in the mediaeval period. Kersey was again affected by the plague in the 1660s. Could the boys have travelled back to Restoration England rather than the time of Edward III or one of his immediate successors? The finished church could have simply been hidden by fully grown trees. Some, however, dispute this later date and point out that Kersey had become rich due to the mediaeval wool trade. It was, therefore, possible that the residents could have afforded glass at a much earlier date than supposed.

I am inclined to believe that the boys did find themselves briefly in an earlier age on that autumn day in 1957. It could have been mediaeval England or the 1660s.

Is time not as we imagine? Some have suggested that the past, present and future are more closely linked than we think. Can certain conditions allow us to travel backwards or even forwards in time? Are some ghosts actually living people from the past or future who have briefly interacted with our own time? Some have even speculated that UFOs are craft from our own future, briefly interacting with the present. And can some disappearances be attributed to the person being lost in another age, never being able to return to their own time?

Laing reflected on their experience and pondered to Mackenzie, *'I wondered if we'd knocked at a door to ask a question who might have answered it? It doesn't bear thinking about.'*

William Laing was right. It does not bear thinking about. If they had, I could now very well be writing about the mysterious disappearance of three boys in 1957 …

CHAPTER EIGHT
LONDON'S HAUNTED CHURCHES

London is regarded as the most haunted city on earth. With over 2000 years of history, it is hardly surprising that every part of the old city centre seems to have a tale or two connected with the supernatural. London's churches are no exception as we have already seen in an earlier chapter. But St James Garlickhythe is not the only haunted church in London as you will soon discover.

ST ANDREW-BY-THE-WARDROBE, QUEEN VICTORIA STREET

The original church dates from the 13th century and was the parish church of William Shakespeare during his time working at the nearby Blackfriars Theatre. The building was destroyed during the Great Fire of London of 1666 and was replaced by a new church which

was designed by Sir Christopher Wren in the baroque style. The church again suffered damage during World War Two but was rebuilt and rededicated in 1961. The curious name of the church is due to it having been sited near the building which was used to house the state robes of the reigning monarch.

The church houses a 15th-century bell, known as Gabriel, which once hung in the tower of Avenbury church in Herefordshire. It held an evil reputation as it was known to ring of its own accord whenever a vicar died there. Witnesses testified that they had heard it on the

St Andrew-by-the-Wardrobe.

65

deaths of the last two vicars before the church was demolished in the 1930s. The bell was then brought to its current home in the city. Roughly a year after being brought to St Andrew's, it was heard to toll at a time when the church was locked. The police were called but they could find no signs of forced entry. It emerged that the vicar of Avenbury had died that very night.

The bell was cracked during the Blitz of 1941 and now lies forever silent on the floor of the church.

ST MAGNUS THE MARTYR, LOWER THAMES STREET

St Magnus is one of London's loveliest churches. It stands on the original alignment of London Bridge and was the only way of entry into London from those heading from the south. It was destroyed in the Great Fire and is regarded as one of Wren's most expensive churches, as the rebuild cost over £9,000.

The building can lay claim to at least one ghost. A figure of a stooping and cowled man has been seen by visitors. Peter Underwood wrote in *Haunted London* of a church worker who saw the figure on three separate occasions. She saw it twice as she was sewing in the vestry. The first time it walked around her and vanished into a wall. The second occasion, some four years later, was more dramatic as it appeared standing next to her. It was so close that she could even see the serge material of the cassock. She looked up and saw that it had no face. It was hardly surprising that she fled the room upon seeing this. The apparition's third appearance occurred during Mass one Sunday morning. She was putting money in the collection box when she saw a man walk up the nave and into a row behind her. She assumed it was a real priest but suddenly remembered that it looked exactly the same as the apparition she had previously seen in the vestry. She turned around but the figure had vanished. The verger confirmed that no one had entered the church during the service.

St Magnus the Martyr.

An electrician working in the church also saw a priest in a serge cassock. The priest appeared to be watching the man intently before he vanished.

One Easter, a man in the choir informed the rector that he had seen a robed figure on the stairs. The figure had then vanished into a wall.

A former rector, the Rev. H. J. Fynes-Clinton, told Underwood that he too had seen the priest after a Sunday service. The congregation had left and the doors had been locked. He was putting some items in a cupboard behind the side altar when he saw a robbed figure about four or five feet in front of him. He was about to ask how he had entered the locked church when the figure stooped down and appeared to be searching for something. The verger asked if he could help. The figure straightened up, looked at him with a smile and vanished.

Another former rector's wife had twice seen a short, black-haired priest kneeling in the Lady Chapel. She described him as wearing an old-fashioned 'sort of cassock'. She turned to speak to him but he disappeared.

Some visitors have seen the figure standing near the site where Miles Coverdale, the person responsible for the first English translation of the Bible, is buried. Others have felt a sense of sadness when standing near the white marble inscription which commemorates him. Miles Coverdale was also the rector of St Magnus and some have wondered if the ghostly figure is him.

A medium in 1951 claimed that the ghost was indeed Miles Coverdale. Apparently, he was unhappy that his remains had been removed to the church after the site of his original burial place, St. Bartholomew-by-the-Exchange, was demolished in 1840.

GREYFRIARS CHURCHYARD, NEWGATE STREET

Another Wren church, Christ Church, was bombed in the Blitz and was never rebuilt. The ruins were turned into gardens and are now a haven for those seeking to escape the hustle and bustle of the surrounding streets.

The churchyard is home to three female ghosts. The first, Queen Isabella of France, was notorious in her day for murdering her husband, Edward II, and ruling England for a time with her lover, Roger Mortimer. Edward III eventually seized power and had Mortimer executed. Isabella was not punished but was never again allowed a say in government. She died in Hertford in 1358 and was buried in the grounds of Christ Church with the heart of her murdered husband on her chest. Her ghost is said to roam the grounds holding her husband's heart.

Elizabeth Barton, the Holy Maid of Kent, was executed at Tyburn for unwisely predicting Henry VIII's imminent death after his marriage to Anne Boleyn. Her head was

Christ Church.

placed on London Bridge but her body was buried in Greyfriars. Her unhappy ghost is also said to walk the grounds.

Lady Alice Hungerford is the third of our female phantoms to haunt Greyfriars. It is alleged that she was executed at Tyburn in 1532 for poisoning her husband but records show that he outlived her by several years, being beheaded for treason in 1540. Whatever the reason for her death, Lady Alice's ghost was supposedly seen by a night watchman quarrelling with the spectre of Isabella after the two phantoms had accidentally met in the graveyard. The quarrel became so heated that the man fled in terror.

A phantom dog, described as looking like a greyhound, was frequently seen in the churchyard prior to World War One. It was assumed to be a living creature until a stick and stone were thrown at the animal. Both objects passed right through it. A monkish figure has also been seen hereabouts. It is thought that he is the ghost of one of the Franciscans who founded the monastery here in the 13th century.

ST BARTHOLOMEW THE GREAT, WEST SMITHFIELD

The church was founded by Rahere, a courtier during the time of Henry I. He had made a pilgrimage to Rome but had caught malaria and was near death. He vowed that if he ever got better he would return to England and establish a hospital for the poor. One night, after recovering, Rahere dreamed that St Bartholomew appeared to him and told him to build a church and hospital in Smithfield which then lay on the outskirts of London.

Rahere was buried in the church and his ghost is still said to visit his beloved foundation. Footsteps have been attributed to him and his figure has been seen several times by those working in the building. One lady was arranging flowers but they kept falling over and appeared to even move when she was not looking. She complained to the rector, who explained that Rahere had been standing behind her and *you know how he dislikes women!'*

Another rector, W. F. G Sandwith, was in the church when he saw a cowled man standing in the nave. He appeared to be examining one of the Norman columns. He walked towards the figure and asked if he needed assistance as the main body of the church was in darkness. The figure ignored him, turned and walked towards the Lady Chapel. The rector followed but as he was about to catch up with the figure it vanished. His wife also saw the same figure standing near the altar rail one Christmas Eve. His face was hidden by a cowl. She spoke to him but he did not answer and then glided into the vestry. She followed him but found the vestry empty. The next day the rector was celebrating Holy Communion when he saw a monk's cowled face looking down at him from one of the pillars. He was so shocked that he paused, and the congregation looking at him with some puzzlement as he did so. He then resumed the service and the face faded away.

St Bartholomew the Great.

Another time, the rector was in the church with two visitors when he saw a monk in a black gown standing in the pulpit. He appeared to be wildly preaching in silence to an invisible congregation, bending to his right and left and thumping cushions in front of him. He noticed that the two ladies appeared unaware of him and made a point of directing their attention to the pulpit, ' *I don't think that pulpit is worthy of the church, do you?'* he said. He also pointed to a Jacobean effigy near the pulpit. Both times they acknowledged what he had pointed out but did not refer to the figure. It was now clear that both ladies could not see the monk. The figure continued preaching in silence for a full 15 minutes before fading away.

Sandwith also recalled a verger and bell ringer called John Hope who had died in St Bartholomew's Close. As he left the dying man he heard a voice call *'Rector'* across the close. He went towards the voice but could find no one. During Hope's funeral service Sandwith noticed the tolling bell had suddenly stopped. It emerged that the rope had snapped as Hope's body had passed by it. During the singing of the psalms, a voice was heard joining in. Sandwith thought that it sounded very much like Hope's.

Elliot O'Donnell once told Peter Underwood that one summer afternoon he had seen a monk pass him as he walked down the aisle. O'Donnell felt that the figure gave the impression of stealth but also noted that it made no sound.

O'Donnell also said that one morning a church official had seen a white luminous shape in the main aisle. It appeared to take the shape of a woman who resembled his daughter, who was then living in Australia. He naturally became very concerned and even thought that she could have died. He later received a letter from her in which she stated that she had been very ill. At one point she believed that she was dying and had thought she was standing in St Bartholomew's looking at her father. It transpired that her father's vision occurred at the same time, allowing for the time difference, as his daughter's experience. The same man also heard footsteps when alone in the church. They were often heard in the ambulatories.

Others have seen a white light or shape in the central aisle. A dark shape was once seen gliding along one of the ambulatories and the curate who witnessed it was so shocked that he became ill for a long time afterwards. Organ music has also been heard when the church has been empty and locked.

Shrieks and groans have been heard outside the entrance to the church. This area was the scene of horrific burnings at the stake in the Tudor period. A grim reminder of these times was discovered in 1849 when, during the digging of a sewer, blackened stones, charred human bones and burnt oak posts were found. Some of the posts still had staples and rings attached to them.

The central aisle was also the scene of a terrifying experience for two ladies one July morning. They began to feel trapped and felt that something evil was following them. This feeling became so intense that they both fled the church. One autumn evening, another female church worker saw something moving by the font. She then saw a small figure wearing a cocked hat who was standing in the shadows by Rahere's tomb. It then vanished. She became convinced that she had seen the ghost of William Hogarth, the painter, who had often frequented the church in his lifetime.

Peter Underwood spoke to a lady, Miss Dorothea St Hill Bourne, who had three strange experiences in the building. Once, she arrived at the church to practice singing Bach. As she sang, she became aware that the church seemed to be filled with a large crowd who were listening to her. As soon as she stopped the impression left her.

She also experienced a time slip on one occasion. She had been walking along one of the ambulatories when she noticed that the altar and candles had moved to a different position to where they normally were. The feeling lasted but a moment before they returned to their normal positions.

She also spoke of a pageant once held in the church and saw a monk walk down the central aisle of the packed church.

In May 1999 the verger, John Caster, received a phone call from the church's security company telling him that the alarms had gone off. He immediately went there but could find nothing to account for the alarms sounding. He then heard the sound of footsteps walking down the central aisle. He asked who was there and the footsteps stopped. They then continued and the verger quickly locked the doors and called the police. The police could find no one. Nor were any windows or doors found to have been opened. The security company sent an engineer the next day to reset the alarms and he was astonished to discover that only the beam near Rahere's tomb had been broken. Whoever had been in the church had apparently suddenly appeared from nowhere.

I had an interesting experience in the church during the 1980s. Upon nearing Rahere's tomb I experienced a sharp pain in my head. As I moved away from the tomb it subsided. I decided to walk back to the tomb and the pain immediately returned. I retraced my footsteps several times and the pain continued to return and subside as I moved to and from the tomb.

Rahere's tomb was opened in 1865 and one of his sandals stolen. The thief became ill and quickly returned the sandal as she thought that she was being punished for the theft. Some believe that Rahere's ghost, if it is indeed he, only became active after this event.

Jack Hallam, the author of *Ghosts of London*, wrote that a correspondent of his was convinced that Rahere's ghost could be seen every 1 July at 7am. He would apparently appear from the Vicar's Vestry and walk around the church.

St Sepulchre-without-Newgate.

ST SEPULCHRE-WITHOUT-NEWGATE

This was another church that was gutted in the Great Fire of 1666 and later rebuilt. The story goes that Sir Christopher Wren was asked to rebuild the building but the church authorities got fed up with waiting and finally did it themselves. During the Blitz, the City Temple church was badly damaged and the congregation moved to St Sepulchre. The vicar informed the minister of the Temple, the Rev. Leslie Weatherhead, that if he happened to see a tall clergyman with a pale face he was not to be alarmed as it was a ghost. The vicar then went on to explain that although he often tried to speak to the figure it never replied to him.

A few weeks later, Weatherhead and his wife invited a friend to dine with them. During lunch, their guest told him that she had seen a *'tall, pale-faced clergyman, with you in the Sanctuary. At first, I thought he was assisting you and then one morning I saw you walk right through him, and I knew he was a ghost.'*

ST GILES-WITHOUT-CRIPPLEGATE, FORE STREET

This building is one of the few mediaeval churches to survive the Great Fire. Oliver Cromwell was married there in 1621 and John Milton was buried near the pulpit in 1674.

The ghost is of relatively recent origin and has been seen in the churchyard since the 1970s. The figure is described as being dark in appearance. Some have suggested that the apparition is a former vicar still loath to leave his home and church.

A grisly tale of 19th-century grave robbery is also connected with the church. The wife of a local parishioner died and was buried in a vault wearing her wedding dress and a valuable wedding ring. The sexton got to hear of this and decided to open the coffin and remove the ring. The ring proved impossible to remove and so he tried to cut off the woman's finger with a knife. You can imagine the thief's surprise when the finger began to bleed and the 'corpse' sat up in the coffin! The sexton fled the scene, leaving his lantern behind in the panic.

The woman was not dead but had been in a coma. The cut had revived her and the lady, after picking up the

St Giles-without-Cripplegate. (Figgis-West)

73

lantern, managed to find her way home where she hammered on the door. A servant appeared and upon seeing his mistress screamed and slammed the door in her face. They naturally assumed they had seen her ghost. The woman's husband was made of sterner stuff and realised his wife was still very much alive. She was brought into the house and eventually made a full recovery. She lived for many years and had several children by her husband. In commemoration of her lucky escape, locals nicknamed her the *Cripplegate Ghost.*

ALL HALLOWS BY THE TOWER, BYWARD STREET

Parts of this church date back to Saxon times and in the crypt can be found the remains of a Roman building and mosaic floor. The church survived the Great Fire and saw Samuel Pepys climb its tower to survey the devastation. The church was gutted during the blitz but was restored to something of its former glory in the 1950s.

In December 1920, a choirmaster and two choirboys went to the church to rehearse. It was 6.20pm and the trio had been singing for about 20 minutes when they saw an elderly, grey-haired woman standing nearby. One of the boys offered her a seat which she accepted by nodding. She was dressed in a rather old-fashioned silk dress, brown shawl and a bonnet tied up under her chin with a black bow. The choirmaster noticed how her eyes *'seemed to burn with a strange radiance. The eyelids did not seem, even for a fraction of a second, to close over them and those staring eyes were fixed on my face as if eagerly searching for something, or as if fascinated by our music.'*

The choirmaster then realised that he had locked the door. How could she have entered the church without making a sound? At 6.45pm the practice ended and turning to switch the main light on he saw that the woman had gone. A scratching sound was then heard from the corner of the rehearsal room. The choirmaster described it as being like that of a cat trying to get out. One of the boys then shouted out that he had seen a black cat rush out of the room and run down the south aisle. A search was made but neither the woman nor the cat could be found. The door to the church was checked. It was still locked.

The following morning a friend of the choirmaster, a writer and clergyman from Cambridge, came to preach at the church. Afterwards, the man asked the choirmaster if he had seen anything unusual during the service? The choirmaster said that he had not.

The clergyman then explained that he had seen a yellow cat come out from under the piano and run around the altar rails as though scared. It then disappeared through some panelling in the east wall of the church.

All Hallows by the Tower. (Figgis-West)

It was later discovered, from an elderly gentleman who was a former choirboy at the church, that a Miss Liscette Rist had been an organist at All Hallows some 60 years before. She had been passionately fond of cats, some of which used to follow her about. She also loved horses and used to scatter sand and ashes on the steep lanes near the church to stop them from slipping. She used to give money to one of the choirboys to feed the local cats and was also very fond of Christmas carols and would often take the boys to sing them in the surrounding lanes and the church itself. It was surmised that the apparition of the lady was her and that the cat was one of the strays she had befriended. Indeed her favourite, a white Persian, often used to sit with her in the church. When it died she asked the church authorities if it could be buried in consecrated ground but they refused. It was believed that she had ignored their refusal and had secretly buried the cat somewhere in the church.

The ghost of the white Persian was seen by Mr Reginald Hill in 1908. He was a choirboy at the church. Once, during a rehearsal, he saw a white Persian cat appear from nowhere and jump on and off the organ stool. The organist, Dr Richardson, had failed to see it. Thirteen years later, in the summer of 1921, Hill returned to the church to visit the then organist Dr Arthur Poyser to discuss the possibility of him visiting Oxford to give advice on music. After their meeting, the organist offered to play one of his new compositions. As he played, Hill noticed a white Persian walk across the organ loft. He stopped Poyser and asked if he had a white cat. Poyser said he did not but was not surprised that it had been seen in the church, '*Oh, that! So you've seen it too, have you?*'

The figure of the organist, if indeed it was her, and the white cat continued to be seen throughout the 20s and 30s. However, no sightings of them have been recorded since the church was damaged during World War Two. It appears that Hitler's bombs finally drove the old lady and her favourite cat from their old home.

ST PAUL'S CATHEDRAL

St Paul's was built on the site of the mediaeval cathedral that was destroyed in the Great Fire. The building that replaced it can lay claim to more than one ghost within its walls. The Kitchener Memorial Chapel is haunted by a figure in old-style clerical clothes. Cathedral staff would find themselves followed by a whistling ghost into the chapel, his whistles increasing as he neared a wall where he would promptly vanish. It was later discovered during repairs to the chapel, following World War One, that a door existed at the point where the phantom disappeared. The door was opened and a long-forgotten stairway was discovered which led to an empty upper room.

Elliot O'Donnell mentions in his *Ghosts of London* book that an American lady and gentleman were visiting the cathedral one summer in 1899. They were walking down the

St Pauls.

central aisle when a 'great black cloud' rose up from the floor in front of them. It appeared to be alive and vanished after rising some 20ft into the air.

O'Donnell also mentions how a lady was in the cathedral when she saw a woman kneeling in front of her. She appeared to be looking for something. The lady decided to ask if the woman needed help and started to walk towards her. As she did so she felt a tap on her shoulder. She turned around but could see no one there. She looked back towards the woman to find that she had gone. A few days later the lady again witnessed the kneeling woman searching for something on the ground and then felt another tap on the shoulder. She was suddenly overcome with an 'eerie feeling' and left the building in a hurry.

CHAPTER NINE
A MOST CURIOUS HAUNTING

London boasts some fascinating ghost stories and the haunting of 8 New Square, Lincoln's Inn, must rank as one of the strangest in the city's long history of paranormal happenings.

The year was 1899 and the third floor of the 18th century house was occupied by the poet Lionel Johnson. He is best remembered today as the author of the poem *The Dark Angel* and for introducing Lord Alfred Douglas to his friend Oscar Wilde, something the poet came to bitterly regret.

The rest of the building was used by lawyers during the day and a caretaker lived in the basement. A separate staircase with its own entrance led to the poet's rooms. The rent had been surprising low due to a number of tenants who had left the building over a period of two years. All had declared that 'weird manifestations' made it impossible for them to continue living there and the landlord had been forced to let the third floor at a much-reduced rate due to its sinister reputation.

Mr Johnson had little more luck than his predecessors and found that 'things happened' there which quite unnerved him. He went on to say to friends that the two rooms off the largest room were the source of the trouble. He finally decided to quit the building in April 1901. He died the following year.

Johnson had mentioned the matter to Ralph D. Blumenfeld, the news editor of *The Daily Mail*. Blumenfeld decided to look into the matter with his friend Max Pemberton, an established author and editor of Cassell's Magazine. Blumenfeld leased the flat after explaining to the landlord's agent of his intention to hold an all-night vigil in the building.

At 11.45 pm on Saturday, 11 May 1901 Blumenfeld and Pemberton found themselves in the empty chambers, now devoid of furniture, curtains and blinds, apart from two chairs and a table in the main room. The pair then proceeded to search the apartment. They locked the main door, latched every window, sealed all the fireplaces and examined every corner. They even sounded the walls to ensure that there were no hidden doors or sliding panels. It was also noted that there was no connection between the smaller rooms except through the principal room. '*Even a black beetle couldn't have escaped unobserved,*' Blumenfeld was later to observe.

The two men then covered the floor of the smaller rooms with powdered chalk to ensure that any footprints or movement would be recorded. The electric light in each room was left on and the door of each was closed. The pair then seated themselves in the main room, the landlord having assured them that this area was unaffected by any strange happenings.

At 12.43am the door of the room on the right suddenly unlatched itself and opened to its fullest extent. The light in the room was still on but nothing could be seen inside to account for the opening. At 12.56am the door of the other room opened.

'*This is unusual!*' said Blumenfeld. Pemberton suggested seeing if the doors would resist their attempts to move them. Both doors moved easily and they wondered if a draft had caused them to move. This explanation was, however, discounted as all the doors, fireplaces and windows were still sealed. They also noted that the chalk dust in both rooms was undisturbed.

At 1.32am the right-hand door clicked and the brass handle was seen to turn. The door opened for a second time, taking some 11 seconds to fully open.

At 1.37am the left-hand door also opened. Three minutes later both doors began to close simultaneously. Eight inches from the frames both doors paused and then slammed shut. The latches were also heard to click.

Between 1.45am and 1.55am, both doors again opened twice, although neither opened simultaneously as before. The doors last opened at 2.07am and 2.09am and it was at this point that Pemberton and Blumenfeld saw indentations in the chalk in both rooms. Something had apparently walked across both rooms!

Looking from both doorways, they found, marked in the chalk powder, the footprints of what appeared to be a bird in the middle of each room. The room to the left contained three footprints and the room to the right contained five. Each print measured two and three-quarter inches in length and appeared to indicate a three-toed bird with a short spur. The prints were clear and distinct and lay diagonally from each door. None of the footprints bore traces of dragging.

Nothing further happened and at 3.30am the two men left the building. Their experiences were published anonymously in *The Daily Mail* on 16 May under the title *A London Ghost – Inexplicable Happenings In Old Chambers*. As you can imagine, the article produced a flood of letters about the case and even the secretary for the *Society for*

Psychical Research, E. T. Bennett, expressed the desire to look into the matter further. For some reason, the SPR never carried out their promised investigation and requests to the newspaper to publish the address of the property were declined for legal reasons and also to deter other would-be investigators.

One curious aspect of this case rarely gets mentioned but is a fascinating tale in itself. On the night of Pemberton and Blumenfeld's investigation, Margaret Verrall, a classics lecturer and spiritualist in Cambridge, was holding a dinner party with some of her female friends at her home at 5 Selwyn Gardens. After her friends had left, she felt the urge to write automatically – a practice in which the person allows a spirit or spirits to write messages through them. The time was 11.10pm and the lady found her writing a message in a mixture of English, Latin and ancient Greek. The message when translated read, '*This is what I have wanted, at last. Justice and joy speak a word to the wise. A.W.V. and perhaps someone else. Chalk sticking to the feet has got over the difficulty. You help greatly by always persevering. Now I can write a name – thus, here it is!*' The rest of the words could not be understood. The message ended with a crude drawing of a bird which Mrs Verrall referred to as '*the cokyoly bird*'.

Mrs Verrall discussed the message with her husband who dismissed it as a joke. However, when she saw a report about the Lincoln's Inn case in the *Westminster Gazette* she was struck by the fact that her message concerning the chalk and the drawing of the bird came less than an hour before Pemberton and Blumenfeld started their investigation. She was inclined to keep an open mind on the matter but did remark, '*In this case, the absurd element in the script and the quaintness of the phrase about the chalk sticking to the feet drew special attention to the writing and it was discussed by us more than once. The word calx is ambiguous; it might mean "heel" as well as "chalk", and it was not until we saw the story in the Westminster Gazette of May 16th that we found an interpretation for the Latin words.*'

Mrs Verrall also dismissed the suggestion of telepathy as the message had been received by her before the appearance of the bird-like footprints in the chalk, '*It is true that the sprinkling of the chalk probably preceded the writing. There is no reason that the writer of the tale had any expectation as to the sort of marks he might find in the chalk; nor did they expect to encounter a bird.*'

So was it all just a strange coincidence or had the medium really connected with an entity haunting 8 New Square?

It is interesting to note that Mrs Verrall later found fame as one of the seven mediums who claimed to be in contact with the spirit of Frederic Myers, one of the founding members of the *Society for Psychical Research*. Each medium received a fragment of a

New Square, Lincoln's Inn.

communication from a spirit claiming to be Myers which made no sense until they were brought together, whereupon they formed a coherent message. The case is still regarded by many as providing one of the most convincing examples of the survival of human consciousness after death.

Twelve years passed and the chambers were occupied by a Charles Appleby. In February 1913 he was found dead in one of the rooms with claw marks on his neck and arms. The windows and doors were found to be sealed and witnesses outside claimed to have seen the barrister fighting with a 'shadowy bird-like creature' which appeared to be as big as the man himself. Another man, John Radlett, also supposedly met a similar end in the building. However, this aspect of the case must be treated with caution as the sole source for these deaths is James Wentworth Day. Although a respected author, he was, as we will see, not above colouring his ghostly accounts with added horror.

Twenty years after the mysterious happenings in Lincoln's Inn, Blumenfeld was asked by a friend if the story was true. He confirmed that it was. *'I don't believe in ghosts one way or the other – but I do know that this thing happened. We both heard what we heard, felt what we felt, and saw what we saw – but don't ask me for an explanation.'*

The mystery of the haunted chambers gradually faded from the public's memory and it was not until the 1950s with James Wentworth Day and Alasdair Alpin MacGregor's retelling of the tale in their books *Ghosts and Witches* and *Phantom Footsteps* that the story again became widely known. MacGregor kept to the facts but Wentworth Day couldn't resist embellishing the story with the claim that a hovering presence of evil had been scnscd by the two men, together with the sounds of a giant bird's wings flapping. This, the author claimed, coincided with the doors and windows of the chambers being flung violently open. If that was not enough, a suitably gruesome illustration of an evil looking owl-like elemental accompanied the piece.

The fact that Lincoln's Inn was the site of numerous public executions has been suggested by some as the possible reason for the haunting. Did the suffering and pain experienced here somehow leave an indelible mark on the surroundings? It is true to say that the area witnessed some particularly horrific executions, including that of Lord William Russell, convicted of plotting to kill King Charles II. Jack Ketch, never the most efficient of executioners, was given the job of dispatching the King's enemy. The first blow with the axe led Russell to cry out, *'You dog, did I give you 10 guineas to use me so inhumanely?'* Three further attempts with the axe from a now very much shaken Ketch were needed to behead him.

The building in New Square is now apparently free of any uncanny disturbances. The strange events of over a 100 years ago are now largely forgotten but will forever remain one of the most puzzling and bizarre cases of ghostly activity on record.

CHAPTER TEN
ROYAL GHOSTS

SANDRINGHAM

The Sandringham estate was purchased by Queen Victoria in 1862 at the request of the Prince of Wales – later Edward VII – as a home for himself and his bride, Princess Alexandra.

The house itself is haunted. Poltergeist activity is said to start every Christmas Eve and continue for several weeks. Footsteps have been heard in the deserted corridors of the servants, quarters. Doors are known to open by themselves and lights often switch themselves on and off. Christmas cards have also moved from one wall to another and bedclothes have been found pulled off the beds.

Heavy breathing noises have also been heard in one room on the second floor and housemaids working in the house even started to refuse to enter it unless accompanied by another servant.

The present Queen once ordered alterations to the old kitchens and it appears that this increased certain activity within the building. A member of the royal family revealed to the

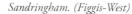

Sandringham. (Figgis-West)

author Joan Forman that a female guest was given a bedroom where she witnessed an apparition. The woman had slept badly and awoke at 2.00am to find the room brightly lit. The door of the bedroom suddenly opened and in came a young boy carrying a long pole. The boy then proceeded to walk around the room, pausing every few seconds to reach up the wall with the pole to light or extinguish long-vanished candles. The female witness was surprisingly unworried by this and watched fascinated until the boy suddenly vanished.

I have often found that alterations to a building can either increase or decrease paranormal activity and this particular sighting sounds very much like a recording that had somehow been activated by the building work.

The library is also the scene of ghostly activity where books have been seen to fly off the shelves. Prince Charles and an aide are said to have had an unpleasant experience when looking for some old prints in this room. They suddenly became extremely cold and felt that someone was standing behind them. They turned round to find no one there. They both left the room in a hurry!

The Queen is apparently fascinated by the ghost stories and is said to be quite open to the possibility of Sandringham being haunted. In 1996 a footman fled the cellars after claiming to have seen the ghost of another servant who had died the previous year. She interviewed him about his experience and was quite impressed by his conviction that he had seen a ghost.

The strangest sighting at Sandringham was made by a footman in his bedroom. He claimed to have seen something like *'a large paper sack breathing in and out like a grotesque lung'*. Not surprisingly, he refused to sleep there after that!

It is not known who or what haunts Sandringham. Queen Alexandra, King George V, Prince Albert Victor and King George VI died there and have all been suggested as being responsible for the ghostly activity.

Or could it be someone else?

Prince Christopher of Greece once claimed to have seen a reflection of a young lady in a black mask in his bedroom mirror. He is said to have described her expression as sad and pleading. This occurred in a room near the clock tower. He later visited Houghton Hall – also in Norfolk – and recognised the lady in a portrait hanging on the wall. The dress and mask matched exactly those worn by the woman in the mirror. It turned out she was a member of the Cholmondeley family who had owned Houghton Hall since the 18th century.

BUCKINGHAM PALACE

One might expect Buckingham Palace to be teaming with ghosts, but any would-be ghost hunter will be sadly disappointed if expecting to run into the spectre of Queen Victoria or any of the other monarchs who have lived and worked there since the 18th century. Only two ghosts have been recorded in the building and one of those pre-dates the palace by several centuries.

The first of our apparitions is a monk who has been seen walking along the grand terrace overlooking the palace gardens. He always appears on Christmas Day and is a decidedly unhappy shade, having been seen bound in chains which clank as he moves. A legend claims that he was held in a punishment cell for breaking the rules of a mediaeval priory which once stood on the site.

Buckingham Palace.

Buckingham Palace's other ghost dates from the 20th century. A certain Major John Gwynne was the private secretary to Edward VII. He became involved in a rather nasty divorce case and so decided to take his life rather than face a scandal in the courts. He shot himself in his first-floor office and since then the sound of a single shot has been occasionally heard in the area where this happened.

WINDSOR CASTLE

The castle and grounds are said to be teeming with ghosts. Windsor's most famous phantom is undoubtedly Queen Elizabeth I. An account from February 1897 concerns her appearance to an officer of the guard whose name was Carr Glynn. He was in the royal library when he heard the sound of heels clicking across wooden boards. Suddenly from the other side of the room, he spotted the figure of a woman. She was dressed in black and had black lace covering her hair. He was very much struck by the figure's resemblance to portraits of Elizabeth I but reasoned that she must be a figure of flesh and blood. She did not appear to notice the guard and walked towards a corner of the room before turning right and appearing to pass into another room. He quickly questioned a library attendant about her but was told that there was no room at the spot where the figure vanished. He also confirmed that he had seen no one enter the room and admitted that others had seen a similar figure in the same area as the officer. It later emerged that in Elizabethan times a flight of stairs did exist which led from that corner of the library to a terrace. Queen Victoria's daughter, the Empress of Prussia and Edward VII are also said to have seen the figure in the library. A tradition states that the Tudor queen also appears during times of war. There are unsubstantiated rumours that George VI saw her several times in September 1939. Rumours persist that a female member of the current royal family has also witnessed her.

It appears that the shade of Elizabeth once shared the library with another royal ghost. George III often stayed at Windsor and his ghost was seen by members of his old guard shortly after his death. The guard was passing the window where their former commander-in-chief used to stand to watch his troops below. They were somewhat surprised to see the unmistakable figure of George III standing there and seemingly very much alive. The commander, without thinking, automatically called out 'Eyes Right'. The figure of the king returned the salute. This appears to have been a one-off haunting as no one has reported seeing him since.

Charles I is reputed to haunt the area of the Canon's House, while Henry VIII is said to walk parts of the castle. Dragging footsteps and groans are said to mark the Tudor monarch's passage through the castle rooms and corridors. Henry's unlucky second wife, Anne Boleyn, also haunts Windsor but apparently steers clear of her former love. She confines herself to the Dean's Cloister. Her tearful face has been seen peering from a window.

In 1936 several spruce trees were removed from the castle grounds at the request of Edward VIII. These had originally been planted by Queen Victoria and her beloved Prince Albert. Workmen at the time claimed to have seen a figure resembling Victoria striding towards them waving her arms and moaning. She was obviously not amused!

One of the most interesting ghost stories connected with Windsor concerns the return of a father to warn his son of impending doom. The story was first reported by the Earl of

Clarendon in his *History of the Rebellion in England*, which he compiled after he fell from Charles II's favour.

The Duke of Buckingham was a favourite of Charles I but was deeply unpopular in the country as he was thought, by many, to have too much influence over the King and affairs of state. In February 1628 an officer of the King's Wardrobe had retired to his bed in the castle only to be confronted by a ghost! The spirit of Buckingham's father, Sir George Villiers, appeared and drew aside the bed curtains. He then instructed the astonished man to warn his son that he was in terrible danger unless he '*did not somewhat ingratiate himself to the people, or at least to abate the extreme malice they had against him*'. The officer was unimpressed as he ignored the warning, assuming it was just a bad dream. The ghost appeared the following night with the same appeal but was again ignored. On the third night, the phantom appeared yet again and the officer finally agreed to pass on the warning after reluctantly conceding that this was no dream. He expressed concern to Sir George that he would not be believed and so the ghost gave him 'two or three particulars' that were only to be mentioned to the duke. The officer travelled to London and managed to gain an audience with Buckingham. History records that the duke, although troubled by the message, failed to heed his father's warning. In August 1628 he was assassinated by a disgruntled subaltern named John Felton.

Other ghosts include several men seen in the early hours of a certain day in April 1906. A Coldstream Guard saw several men descending the steps of the East Terrace. Assuming they were intruders, he shouted a warning which went unheeded by the men,

Windsor Castle.

who continued to walk towards him. He challenged them a further two times before firing his rifle at the first figure. The figures suddenly vanished and the hapless soldier was confined to barracks by his disbelieving superiors.

In 1927 an 18-year-old sentry in the Grenadier Guards shot himself in the Long Walk after becoming depressed by life in the army. A few weeks later, one of his former colleagues, a Sergeant Leake, reported that he recognised the ghost of the young man coming towards him one moonlit night. It emerged that another soldier had also encountered the ghost of the suicide during his patrol of the Long Walk.

The ghost of a policeman haunts part of the castle grounds. He died in the 1940s of a heart attack. The Deanery is haunted by a young boy who shouts, *'I don't want to go riding today'*. His footsteps can also be heard crossing the building. In the Curfew Tower yet more ghostly footsteps are heard on the staircase and the tower bells once swung on their own, which coincided with the temperature in the area suddenly becoming cold. A kitchen in the Horseshoe Cloisters is home to the ghostly figure of a man and horse who walk through a wall. The records for Windsor Castle reveal that the cloisters were once used as stables.

Finally, a possible timeslip occurred in 1873. A night-time visitor to the castle noticed that a group of statues had been erected near St. George's Chapel. They consisted of three standing figures with a fourth crouching down. The central standing figure was holding a large sword. When the visitor later returned to re-examine the group, they had vanished!

CHAPTER ELEVEN
LINCOLN'S HAUNTED HERITAGE

Lincoln was a Roman foundation. The collapse of the Roman Empire saw the town decline but by the mediaeval period it had become one of the most prosperous places in Britain, with an imposing cathedral and castle dominating the skyline. The city continues to prosper to this day and is a centre for tourism, industry and learning. Lincoln is also a very haunted place with a wealth of ghostly stories on record.

LINCOLN CATHEDRAL

The cathedral is one of the finest religious buildings in England. It was founded in 1072 and for over 200 years (1311–1548) was the tallest building in the world. It is the fourth largest cathedral in Britain and is also haunted.

The building's earliest ghost story concerns Bishop Robert Bloet. He died in 1123 and was buried in the cathedral. His ghost was seen wandering about the aisles with 'other walking spretes' and the monks were forced to conduct a series of prayers to banish his restless spirit. The service was not entirely successful as the Bishop's hunting horn is still said to be heard

Lincoln Cathedral. (Jason Figgis)

Lincoln Cathedral at the time of the English Civil War.

in the cathedral from time to time. Another bishop, Henry Burghersh, also haunts the building. He died in 1340 and was said to have appeared to the canons in hunting dress. He demanded that they return parkland in Tinghurst, Buckinghamshire, to the rightful owners. The Bishop could not rest as he had unjustly taken it upon himself to enclose the land just before his death. The canons did as he asked and the ghost was never seen again.

A line of praying monks has been reported in the cloisters and the bells have been heard to ring on their own. A man in 17th-century clothing has also been seen walking up the steps at the front of the cathedral. In the 1960s a lady committed suicide by throwing herself from one of the cathedral towers and her ghost is now said to occasionally re-enact the fateful fall. Another suicide connected with the building concerns the Bishop's Eye window. It is said that most of the work on the window was carried out by an apprentice. His master was working elsewhere in the cathedral but came to inspect the window after it had been finished. He realised that the work was far better than his own and threw himself in despair from the gallery. A stain below the Bishop's Eye is said to mark the spot where he died.

In 2016 there was a flurry of excitement in the press after Paul Jackson, a visitor to the cathedral, posted a video on YouTube. The footage appeared to show a white shape dart

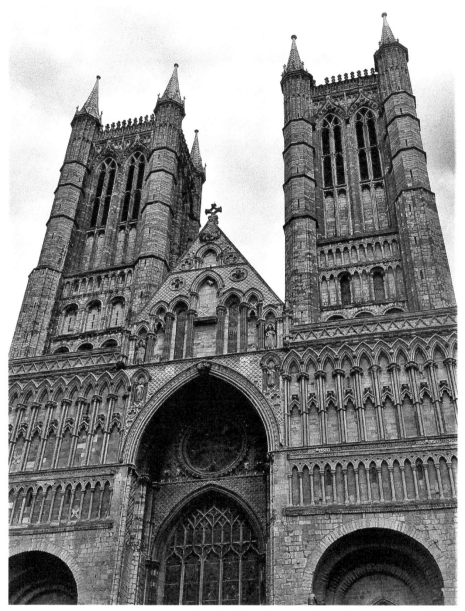

Lincoln Cathedral. (John West)

from right to left across the top of the Willis Organ. However, a closer inspection of the video shows a tour group immediately below the organ. Cathedral guides use torches to highlight interesting features in the building and it is highly likely the white shape is the beam from a torch.

In 2011 a lady called Leah Harrison took a photo of what appeared to be two figures in the cathedral. The figures are too blurred to identify with any certainty but that has not

The Lincoln Imp.

stopped some claiming they are of a woman and a boy in a hat. Others say that one of the figures is a bearded man or cleric.

In the late 1960s the writer David Bridgeman-Sutton was in a London club with his friend David Rutter, the canon and precentor of Lincoln Cathedral. The canon suddenly became agitated and said that something was wrong at Lincoln. He said that he must ring the cathedral and rushed out to find a phone. The canon soon returned and told his friend that the dean of the cathedral had collapsed and died earlier that day.

The Lincoln Imp sits on a pillar in the Angel Choir. A 14th-century legend claims that the Devil sent two imps to England to cause trouble. They visited Chesterfield where they twisted the tower of the church before heading to Lincoln where they entered the cathedral. They tripped up a bishop, blew out the candles, smashed windows and set about breaking up the furniture. An angel appeared and ordered them to stop. One of the imps started throwing stones at the angel and was promptly turned into stone as a punishment for his shocking behaviour. The other imp, realising that the game was up, fled back to the Devil. The imp is now a symbol of the city and replicas and souvenirs bearing his image are sold in their thousands every year.

Queen Anne's Well lies not far from the cathedral. The door to the covered well has six holes in it. A curious legend states that if you walk around the well seven times and then put a finger in one of the holes you will be judged by the Devil. If you only feel his breath, you will be fine. If he bites off your finger, you can expect a place in Hell when you die!

GREESTONE STEPS

The Black Death ravaged Britain in the 1300s. Lincolnshire was not spared and many thousands died. A mass grave was dug by the cathedral, near the top of Greestone Steps, and hundreds were buried there.

Legend states that once a year, on the anniversary of their internment, their singing spirits leave the graves and march towards an entrance at the cathedral known as the Judgement Porch. They are then judged by Mary and Jesus to see if they are worthy to go inside.

A figure of a clergyman wearing a long cloak and hat is also said to haunt the steps. He supposedly hanged himself from the Postern Gate and now remains in the area to guide

Greestone Steps. (Figgis-West)

weary travellers up the steep steps to the cathedral. Three nurses claimed to have seen him before he vanished through a solid wall. They described his clothes as looking as if they dated from the 1600s.

Cameras sometimes malfunction at the gate and photos often show strange specks of light. Noises have been heard coming from the arch and in December 2013 a photo was taken by Kaya Jordan Otley during a ghost walk. The picture, taken on a mobile phone, appeared to show a shadowy human-like figure standing beneath the arch.

Another photo was taken by Dawn Scargill at the top of these steps in April 2006. She was ghost hunting with her twin sister, Tracy, and took the picture at approximately 9.42pm. The image of a white, misty shape – some claim it shows a horse and rider – appeared on one of the stills.

In the early 1990s a young lady was climbing the steps one summer evening when suddenly the temperature dropped as she reached Greestone Place. She then saw the apparition of a woman in long robes, like those of a nun or nurse, carrying a baby. She was floating several inches above the ground. The figure then turned into Greestone Terrace and vanished. The woman fled in terror and refused to ever use the steps again. A building in a courtyard, opposite Greestone Terrace, was once a hospital and it is thought that the ghost may be connected with it.

A house in Greestone Place is also haunted. During World War Two, the inhabitants of one of the homes here reported hearing noises in the early hours of the morning 'like the sound of large trunks being thrown about'. A search of the building revealed no explanation for the noises. The couple were so terrified that they rushed outside in their nightclothes.

Jenny Bright and Dr David Cross, the authors of *Ghosts of Lincoln*, wrote of an odd experience on the steps. It was an early April evening in 1995 and the pair were preparing for a ghost walk. They suddenly noticed the sound of footsteps following them. They stopped and so did the footsteps with 'a sort of brief sliding sound'. This happened three times in all. There was no one else on the steps and they were unable to provide an explanation for what they heard.

However, the most bizarre haunting associated with the steps is a bouncing head! St Hugh was a French nobleman, Benedictine and Carthusian monk and Bishop of Lincoln. He was made a saint in 1220 and was once the best-known English saint after Thomas Beckett. He is the patron saint of shoemakers, the sick and swans.

After his death, his remains were kept in Lincoln Cathedral in a chest full of gold and jewels. One evening, two thieves hid in the building and stole the chest after the cathedral had closed. They took their booty down Greestone Stairs but slipped and dropped the chest as they made their escape. The contents, including the skull, fell out across the steps. The thieves were soon caught and the chest was returned to the cathedral. Since then, the apparition of St Hugh's head can be seen rolling down the steps. To make matters worse, it sometimes hits the backs of people's legs who are walking before it!

LINCOLN CASTLE

The castle was founded by William the Conqueror in the 11th century. It later became a prison and court and was the scene of many executions during the 18th and 19th centuries. The gravestones of some of the executed prisoners can still be seen in the Lucy Tower.

The prison chapel is haunted by unexplained lights and doors open and close by themselves. Some visitors have sensed unseen figures in the coffin-like pews. Cobb Hall – the scene of public executions from 1817 to 1859 – is home to a woman in black who walks up and down the stairs which lead to the site of the gallows on the roof. She once tried to push a girl down the stairs but the child was saved by her father, who then saw the woman vanish into thin air. The mother later said that as she walked past the Cobb Hall she would hear a voice calling her to enter the tower alone.

Some visitors to the tower have claimed to have heard the sounds of footsteps, the crank of a lever and the opening of the gallows trapdoor on the roof.

Lincoln Castle. (John West)

Crying and groaning noises have been reported in the Lucy Tower and the female prison is haunted by a woman in Victorian clothing who carries a baby. The male prison is haunted by the jangling of keys, screams, groans, footsteps and doors slamming.

Some people climbing the Observatory Tower have experienced a feeling of fear and nausea upon reaching the top. In 2004 one family caught a white, misty shape on camera as they made their way back down the winding stairs.

In 1992 a man in his early 20s was walking up Steep Hill. He reached Castle Hill and started to make his way towards Bailgate. He was shocked to see a black horse suddenly appear. Its rider was wearing a cloak and was heard to shout *'Open the gates! Open the gates!'* The horse and rider galloped towards the castle entrance and promptly vanished. Since then, others have also claimed to have heard the sounds of a horse galloping towards the castle gate in the early hours of the morning.

BROWN'S PIE SHOP

Brown's Pie Shop on Steephill dates from the 1400s but was rebuilt in the 17th century. It was once a pub known as the Fox and Hounds and T. E. Lawrence (also known as Lawrence of Arabia) stayed here while serving at RAF Cranwell. It was at this time that he wrote his book *Seven Pillars of Wisdom*. The Pie Shop is now a restaurant and is also home to a ghost known as Humphrey.

Simon was the head chef in the building. He worked in the kitchen on the first floor and would often feel that he was being watched. He felt that the presence was that of a child and nicknamed him Humphrey. A fire blanket was once thrown at the chef and so he took to calling out a greeting to Humphrey upon arriving each morning for work. This seemed to please the ghost and all returned to normal.

One morning, Simon was ill and the manager opened the restaurant in his place. He was not aware of the greeting and so the ghost did not get his morning welcome. The manager set to work in the kitchen chopping vegetables but had to go downstairs to answer the phone. Upon returning to the kitchen, he was in for a shock. The knife that he had been using was stuck in the floor. It was still waving and was several feet from where the manager had left it. It was as if Humphrey was venting his anger at being ignored!

Simon once found himself working alone early one morning during the time of Lincoln's famous Christmas market. He was busy in the kitchen when he suddenly heard the front door slam. He knew the door was locked and ran down expecting to find that someone had broken in. He found the door firmly secure and the keys on the floor despite having left them in the lock. He was so scared by this that he went home and only returned in daylight.

On another occasion, the chef heard the sounds of coins being counted in the office on the second floor. Assuming that the manager was there, he climbed the stairs and looked in. He was shocked to see several coins suspended in the air. They then fell to the floor with a crash. It is hardly surprising to learn that the chef again fled the building in some shock.

One of the rooms upstairs has the name 'W. Bailey' scratched into a windowpane. Cold spots have been felt in this room and the staff prefer to avoid this part of the building as they feel that they are being watched.

A woman with psychic abilities was once eating in the restaurant. She explained to the staff that she enjoyed her food but had been somewhat distracted by the ghostly boy who constantly stood near her table and watched her eat!

THE STRUGGLERS INN

The Strugglers Inn lies beneath Lincoln Castle. Its unusual name refers to the hangings carried out in the castle. Indeed, the pub sign features a condemned man having his hands tied on the scaffold.

When public hangings were considered a useful deterrent, people used to gather at the pub and watch. The pub is haunted and has experienced some poltergeist activity with objects disappearing and beer glasses flying off the shelves.

The pub is also home to a phantom dog. He was the companion of William Clark who was executed in the castle in 1877 for murdering Henry Walker, a gamekeeper. After Clark had been arrested, his dog would wander around the castle grounds and also the pub

The Strugglers Inn. (Figgis-West)

where his master used to drink. It is said that at the moment of Clark's death, the lurcher became rigid, lifted its head and howled. The abandoned dog was finally taken in by the landlord who felt sorry for it. When it died, he decided to have the animal stuffed and displayed in the pub. It later ended up on display in the castle.

The ghost of the lurcher has been heard barking, whining and scratching at the pub's front door on several occasions. People have also reported feeling a dog brush past them. It has also been seen sitting by the bar and is also supposed to haunt the castle ramparts where it still searches for its owner.

THE WHITE HART

There has been an inn on this site since the 14th century but the oldest part of the current building dates back to 1710.

In the 18th century, a highwayman once tried to hold up a coach on the road to Lincoln but had a burning torch thrust into his face by the coachman. The highwayman was left to die in agony as the coach sped on to the White Hart. Another version of the tale states that the highwayman was killed by some soldiers in the coaching yard. The ghost of the highwayman has been seen in the Orangery (the site of his death) on several occasions. He hides his terrible scars by holding a cloak up to his face but was also once seen in one of the corridors without his cloak. His face was described by the witness as black with lifeless eyes. A smell of leather and horse sweat also accompanied his appearance.

Two ladies, Margaret and Catherine, were staying in the hotel two weeks before Christmas. They were in the city to set up a new branch of a travel agents. They were both disturbed late one night by the sounds of a boy and an older girl playing on the stairs and in the corridor. The children then appeared to enter one of the other bedrooms on the same floor where they continued to play loudly. The next morning, one of the ladies complained to the receptionist about the noise and asked to speak to the parents. The receptionist told them that no children were staying in the hotel. She also confirmed that no other rooms in their corridor were occupied at that time.

A crying, cowering girl in a mop-cap and apron haunts the landing on the stairs in the north-east corner of the building. She was murdered by the hotel's drunken rat-catcher after resisting his advances.

A previous owner of the hotel, dressed in smoking jacket and cravat, haunts his old rooms overlooking Bailgate. He cries out '*please help me find my ginger-jar*' before vanishing. He was robbed of a valuable antique jar during his time at the hotel and continues to search for it even in death. A man sadly committed suicide in the hotel in the 1960s.

The White Hart Hotel. (Figgis-West)

People have commented on the feeling of sadness in the room where he died. Sobbing and a loud explosion like a gunshot has also been heard in the room.

A tabby cat was once seen to run up a corridor and pass through the closed door of a second-floor bedroom. A man in 17th-century clothes lurks in the passages below the hotel and another man in a 19th-century military uniform has been spotted on the top floor.

In the 1960s kitchen staff saw a patch of light flitting around the empty restaurant for some 20 minutes. This light had also appeared several years before when a couple were having a meal in the restaurant. To make matters worse, their cutlery and plates were also moved about by an unseen force.

In the 1980s the son of the hotel proprietors told his parents that he had been tucked into bed by a lady in a long flowing dress. The boy showed no fear at this and calmly accepted his bedtime visitor. He even drew a picture of her for his startled parents. Is this the same ghost as the old lady in the 19th-century clothes who haunts the lower corridors? She always vanishes if approached.

Finally, some guests have reported hearing the sounds of marching feet outside the hotel. Others have also heard the clatter of wheels and horses' hooves on the cobbles below.

THE THEATRE ROYAL

The current theatre was built in 1893 on the site of an earlier theatre which had been destroyed by fire the year before. Sir Patrick Stewart made his professional debut as an

The New Theatre Royal. (Figgis-West)

actor here and the theatre was popular with the RAF during World War Two – Guy Gibson of Dambusters fame was a regular attendee.

In 1974, during an afternoon performance, Martin, a member of staff looked up into the circle and noticed a plump man with a large moustache smoking a cigar on the back row. This area was not in use during this performance and the man should not have been sitting there. Smoking was also not allowed and Martin went up to ask the man to put his cigar out. When he reached the seat where the man had been sitting, he found that he had vanished. He searched the area but could not find him. He noticed that the seat was down – unoccupied seats were always left up – and there was no trace of cigar smoke. It would have been impossible for the man to have left the circle without a member of staff seeing him. A further search of the area revealed a blocked-up doorway close to where the man had been sitting. Had the figure been a ghost and had it vanished through the blocked door? It is hardly surprising that this area of the theatre later became known as the 'haunted corner'.

In 1994 several theatre staff saw another figure in the circle. It later emerged that no one had been in that part of the theatre at the time the phantom had been seen. Footsteps have been heard in the lounge area. They sound as if they are walking on a wooden floor despite the area now being carpeted. The area above the stage, known as The Flies, is also haunted. Stagehands once heard noises coming from there. They rushed upstairs but could find no one. They returned to their duties, upon which the noises started up again.

Paul was the chief designer at the Theatre Royal. It was around 3am and he was working alone in the building on some designs for new scenery. He left the stage to view his work from the front row of the circle when he suddenly saw the curtain come down. He assumed that the ropes had not been secured properly. As he made his way back to the stage, the curtain suddenly went up again! This action could not have happened on its own and he shouted out '*Who's there?*' He then ran to the stage but could find no one. He also found the curtain ropes were securely tied up.

A ghostly figure was once seen climbing a ladder backstage. It vanished after a member of staff called out to it. One of the dressing rooms at the top of the theatre is reported to be haunted. One young actress ran screaming from it after claiming to have seen 'something.' She left the production and never returned.

An electrician was working in the auditorium when he heard a strange noise coming from one of the seats. He found it impossible to accurately describe what he had heard. Another electrician also heard the same noise coming from the same area of the building. He also could not find words to accurately describe the sounds. Both men declined to work in the theatre again after their experiences.

On another occasion, the staff heard a bang coming from the auditorium. They ran to investigate and found all the seats down as if occupied by an unseen audience. Some members of staff have also felt someone tap them on the shoulder when no one has been near them.

In my book, *Britain's Haunted Heritage*, I wrote about the Theatre Royal in Bath and the phantom butterflies which only appear if the production is due to be a success. The Theatre Royal in Lincoln also has a butterfly tradition. Several different species have been seen and they only appear during the pantomime season and only if the production is successful. They flit across the stage before vanishing into the wings. They are never seen anywhere else in the theatre and searches for them, after they have flown off stage, always prove fruitless.

THE GREEN DRAGON

This pub lies next to the River Witham. Parts of it date back to the 1600s, although it was heavily restored in the mid-20th century. The building is haunted by the ghost of an old woman. In the early 1990s a barmaid once saw her in a function room on the top floor. She described her as being very short, some four and a half feet in height and was wearing a grey and black striped shawl. She was also smoking a clay pipe. The girl was so scared by her experience that she quit her job immediately.

The Green Dragon. (Figgis-West)

The landlord at the time of this sighting was Andy McLaren. In December 1994 he was chatting to two ladies who were sitting in the bar. They told him that they used to live in the building before it was renovated. They also said that Mary Cooper, the grandmother of one of them, had run a second-hand clothing shop in part of what became the pub. She had acquired the nickname of '*Umbrella Mary*' after becoming well-known in the city for making and selling umbrellas.

They explained that Mary had lived above the shop but had died not long after it had been renovated. The landlord asked the two ladies if they had experienced any paranormal activity during their time in the building. They said no, explaining that they had found the place to be peaceful and free of any ghostly activity. Andy then asked for a description of the old lady. They explained that illness as a child had caused Molly to have a curved spine which had left her only four and a half feet tall. She always wore an Irish shawl in winter. It was grey with broad, black stripes. She also smoked a dojeen which they explained was a type of clay pipe. The landlord realised that the description matched exactly that of the figure seen by the barmaid a few years before.

One Halloween, the landlord was relaxing on a sofa after he had locked up the pub for the night. The time was around 11.40am. He was suddenly disturbed by the sounds of a party coming from the locked and empty Witham Suite. The sounds of talking and laughing were quite distinct but as the clock started to strike midnight all became quiet again.

The Witham Suite also experienced poltergeist activity. Staff would often leave the empty room and upon returning would find tables and chairs moved from where they had left them. On one occasion, a table had been put next to the entrance. One member of staff placed a pile of leaflets on the table and then left to do something else. When they returned, the leaflets were found thrown across the room. This could not have been caused by a draft as all the doors and windows were shut.

The cellars are also haunted. Staff would often hear the sounds of barrels and crates of beer being dragged about. A search found the cellars to be empty, although it was noted that some of the barrels and crates had been moved.

Autumn 1994 saw a new gas system, which controlled the pumping of the bar, installed in the cellar. During one busy session at the pub, the beer taps suddenly stopped. The landlord assumed that the gas cylinder was faulty and sent the barman down to change it. He soon reappeared looking somewhat worried. He asked the landlord to come with him and a search of the cellar found every barrel tap turned off. The cellar had been locked at the time and it would have impossible for anyone to have gained access to it.

An all more sinister event occurred one Sunday morning in 1995. One of the kitchen staff was cutting beef with a carving knife when they were called to the phone. They left the knife on the chopping board, but upon returning to the kitchen, found the knife snapped in two and placed in an X shape on the board.

The Castle Hill Club. (Figgis-West)

At the time of writing, the Green Dragon is empty. One can only wonder if the ghost of the old lady will be seen again when the pub finally finds a new buyer.

THE BOTTOM PINCHER

The Castle Hill Club below the castle was originally called the Black Boy Inn. Isambard Kingdom Brunel, the engineer, and William Marwood, the public executioner, once stayed here. Both men are said to haunt the building and Marwood has been seen gazing out from one of the upper windows. The club is also home to another ghost – unless it is one of the gentlemen mentioned above – who likes to pinch the bottoms of both staff and drinkers in the bar. The phantom bottom pincher is not choosy about who it accosts and is happy to pinch the bottoms of either sex!

CHAPTER TWELVE
SCOTLAND'S ROAD OF HORROR

The A75 between Gretna and Dumfries in Scotland has a sinister reputation with tales of strange apparitions that date back to at least the 1950s. Many of the recorded incidents have taken place along the old A75 – now the B721 – with the section between Annan and Gretna being a particular hotspot for paranormal activity.

In 1955 Jim Carlyle was driving a taxi from Eastriggs to Annan. His girlfriend was in the passenger seat. The figure of a woman in white, wearing a long cape, suddenly floated across the road in front of them. He braked hard but the car went through the apparition. It is not recorded if his girlfriend also saw the figure.

Andrew Green, the author of several books on ghosts, mentions a sighting from October 1957. A lorry driver called Hugh Watson Reid was driving towards Carlisle. The time was 10.45pm and he had reached a bend in the road near Sark Bridge, at the junction with the A75, when a middle-aged couple walked arm in arm in front of his vehicle. The man was described as wearing tight trousers, a high tile hat and a short double-breasted jacket. The woman was wearing a large hat and a crinoline ankle-length gown. Reid pulled up and put his hazard lights on. He then got out to complain to the couple but found to his surprise that they had vanished into thin air. The road was bordered by a high hedge at this spot which seemingly ruled out the couple escaping across the fields. Green also mentions that other night drivers had seen the same couple. He also speaks of a ghost car, its lights dipped, which suddenly disappears along this stretch of road. One couple and their two children were almost killed when their car ended up in a ditch after the phantom car drove towards them before suddenly vanishing.

In 1960 – some sources place the sighting in the 1990s – Margaret Ching and her fiancée were approaching Skew Bridge in the early hours of the morning when they saw an old woman in Victorian clothes standing in the centre of the road. They were unable to stop in time and the car appeared to pass right through her. A dramatic drop in temperature was felt by the couple as they did so.

The haunted road. (Figgis-West)

A night in April 1962 was never to be forgotten by Derek and Norman Ferguson. The two brothers, aged 22 and 14, were travelling home after touring Scotland in their father's saloon car. They had stopped for petrol in Dumfries and then found themselves heading towards Annan along the A75.

It was near midnight and the moon was shining brightly. Derek remarked on how deserted the road appeared when a large hen suddenly flew towards the windscreen of the car. Derek swerved to avoid it and the bird vanished just before it hit them. The brothers had barely enough time to recover when the figure of an old woman, waving her arms in the air, rushed out towards them. She also vanished as the car was about to hit her. But worse was to follow. Goats, large dogs, cats, large fowl and a screaming old man with long hair appeared from nowhere as the car continued along the road. The car swerved from side to side to avoid the approaching apparitions, none of which made contact with the vehicle. Derek started to think that he was hallucinating but his brother's terrified look confirmed that he was seeing the same things too.

The temperature in the car dropped noticeably. As Derek later recalled, *'My hands seemed to become very heavy and it was as if some force were trying to gain control of the steering wheel; the control of the car became increasingly difficult. We seemed to be suffocating and I opened the window to get some fresh air but it was bitterly cold outside and I just hung on to the wheel as screaming, high-pitched laughter and cackling noises seemed to mock our predicament. I was absolutely certain at the time that an attempt was being made to force us off the road and I was equally certain that a fatal accident would result.'*

Derek decided to pull over. As he did so, the car started to rock violently and bounced up and down so much that the pair felt dizzy. Derek, feeling sick, opened the car door and jumped out. As he did so, the car stopped shaking and became quiet. When Derek returned to the car, the violent rocking and shaking started up again as if fists were striking the vehicle. A high wind also blew up and strange laughter sounded all around them. Derek also noted that his brother was strangely quiet during this ordeal.

Derek started up the car and continued to drive slowly down the road. The weird apparitions continued to appear, leaping in front of the vehicle and vanishing just before impact was certain. The brothers then noticed a small red light in front of them. It soon became apparent that it was the rear light of a slow-moving furniture van. Derek suddenly found that he was unable to remove his foot from the accelerator pedal as the car sped towards the lorry. He also tried to swerve but found that he could not move the wheel. He screamed to his brother to prepare for a crash when the van suddenly vanished!

The brothers drove on towards Annan, the speed of their car now reduced to a crawl. The whole terrible experience had lasted for almost half an hour and Derek thanked himself for filling up the petrol tank at Dumfries. He shuddered to think what could have happened if the car had run out of petrol when they had been surrounded by the terrifying apparitions.

Derek later spoke to a friend who had seen military service near Annan during World War Two. It emerged that witchcraft was rumoured to have been practised in the area. Another friend also spoke of the ghostly furniture van being seen at other times on the road.

Peter Underwood, the author of a book on haunted Scotland, spoke to the brothers about the case and wondered if Norman, then aged 14, had provided the unconscious link with the terrible figures seen that night? The brothers later moved to Spain and proved untraceable when Underwood wanted to go over some further points about the case.

In the 1970s a man and a woman were seen on the road. The man was described as missing his eyes. The couple were similar in appearance to the figures seen by Jim Carlye in 1955.

In the early 1990s an unnamed taxi driver and his wife were driving to Collin along the Dumfries bypass when a woman in green appeared by the roadside. She walked out into the road as the car neared her and the couple braced themselves for a crash. The figure then vanished. The couple searched for her without success.

In 1995 Garson and Monica Miller were heading towards Annan on the Kinmount Straight when a man in a cloak jumped out in front of their car. He was described as looking like a monk and was holding out a sack. They thought that they had hit the man but a search revealed no signs of impact. They even reported the incident to the Annan police.

In 1997 Donna Maxwell was travelling along the old A75 with her two children. They all saw a man in his 30s, dressed in dark trousers and a red top, jump out in front of the car. She slammed on her breaks but the expected crash never came. She reported the matter to the local police. Other drivers have also reported seeing the same man standing by the road.

The evening of 12 December 2010 saw Derek McCall driving on the western fridges of Dumfries when the figure of an elderly woman appeared by the road and walked out in front of him. He hit the brakes and the apparition vanished. He was doing 60mph at the time and should have hit her if she had been a living person.

In March 2004 a woman was driving home at night when she forced to stop after seeing a stagecoach and horse cross the road in front of her. She described it as 'like a grainy fuzzy picture you'd see on an old black & white TV'. The apparition vanished after ten seconds. It is interesting to note that her partner phoned her immediately after the incident feeling that she had been involved in a crash.

An undated report speaks of a person waiting in a broken-down car at the Annan – Cummertrees junction. They saw a pair of legs taller than the car run past them into nearby woods. The legs were not attached to a body!

Another undated sighting concerns a taxi driver who was travelling to work one morning along the Kinmount Straight. It was foggy and he had reduced his speed as a precaution. He had just reached a point where trees bordered both sides of the road when he saw a bear-like creature cross in front of him from left to right. He looked back and saw that the 'bear' had turned into a woman.

In 2013 Bob Sturgeon, the owner of a roadside snack van at Carrutherstown, spoke to BBC Scotland about the road. He believed the road to be haunted and said that '*There was very rarely a week went past without somebody telling me about some experience and usually along that Kinmount straight.*'

He also said that traumatised lorry drivers often sought refuge at his van after seeing things on the road. Drivers would see groups of dejected-looking people pulling handcarts or carrying bundles '*like some mediaeval camp followers*'.

One driver was so affected by his experience that he gave up lorry driving and was never seen again. According to Bob Sturgeon, the man '*had been parked on the Kinmount straight and he had woken up at the back of three in the morning and he saw this "parade" of people. He said that it went on for ages and he had just frozen – he was in an awful state.*'

Strange sightings along stretches of the A76 continue to this day.

CHAPTER THIRTEEN
TALES FROM A GHOST HUNTER'S NOTEBOOK

THE WALKING DEAD?

The author and ghost hunter Thurston Hopkins once had an interesting encounter in late Victorian London. He was friends with the poet Ernest Dowson and the pair often found themselves indulging in a game known as 'blind chivvys' where they sought out short cuts to experience a London of forgotten alleys, lanes and courtyards.

It was the last blazing hot day in August and the two were turning into an alley when Hopkins caught sight of an indistinct figure which seemed to be following them. He hugged the walls and appeared to be in some haste, almost as if he desired to catch up with them but could not. Hopkins made Dowson aware of the figure and they both decided to shake off their unwanted companion by dodging down alleys and zigzagging across the narrow courts. Despite this, the figure still managed to stay with them and Hopkins and Dowson became alarmed about the man's intentions.

Dowson commented to Hopkins: '*There's something about the motion of that thing which gives me the creeps. It's so dummy-like and yet so full of some fiendish and vital force. We will do well to see that he does not approach too close to us.*'

They both then decided to run and soon found themselves in Tottenham Court Road, the figure lost in the crowds that now surrounded them.

A few days later, Hopkins and Dowson were in a restaurant by Charing Cross Station when they were horrified to see the same man who had followed them suddenly appear at the doorway. He was tall, thin and wore an old overcoat with a mackintosh thrown over it. His face was covered by an old, dirty silk scarf which was bound round his jaw and in his hand was an old Gladstone bag.

Dowson had been looking for his cigarette case at the time the figure appeared and was quite shaken when the man approached him and said, '*Try your hip pocket.*' Dowson reluctantly did so and to his amazement found the missing case. The man then looked at

Ernest Dowson.

the pair and both were immediately filled with a sense of fear and revulsion at his almost mummified appearance. It was the man's face that appalled them more than anything. Hopkins was struck by his unearthly appearance, finding it difficult to even regard him as a living being. Dowson later remarked how the man's face '*reminded him of a wizened bladder of lard*'. It was hardly surprising that they quickly finished their drinks and fled.

The encounter with the mummy-like figure was largely forgotten until one evening when the two were walking towards a house in Euston Road where Dowson lodged. They were about 100 yards from the building when they again saw the sinister figure with the Gladstone bag. Both were suddenly filled with a sense of evil, and to make matters worse the man was walking up the steps to Dowson's lodgings! Upon seeing this, Dowson quite understandably declined to spend the night there and stayed with a friend instead.

It was to be several days before Dowson could be persuaded to return home. Upon entering the building he noticed that his landlady was very agitated . He asked her what had happened and she explained that a man who had given his name as Lazarus had rented one of the rooms for a week. He had been found dead the next day. The police were called and a search of his body found that his only possession was an old battered Gladstone bag. It was opened and was found to contain nothing but earth! Further enquiries proved fruitless and the man's exact identity or origins remained a mystery.

Dowson later told Hopkins that he was convinced that the man was not of flesh and blood. *'Let me tell you something, Hopkins. That mould in his bag was graveyard mould ... And was it not Lazarus that had been dead that did come forth from his grave bound in a winding sheet and his face bound with a napkin?'*

Hopkins often wondered about that strange figure with the Gladstone bag. Had he and Dowson been too quick to judge the man? Had he just been a harmless and eccentric vagrant? But as time went on Hopkins became convinced that the man had been dying on his feet and had been seeking out someone to take pity on him. Had the pathetic figure been dead at the time of their first encounter? Hopkins came to believe that by some strange power the man's soul had been able to stay in control of his dead body until that day in the lodging house when it was forced or decided to leave the corpse and embark on that final journey that all of us must ultimately make.

THE MAN IN THE FOG

The year was 1917 and Henry Kirkup, a sergeant on leave, was heading for Newcastle Central Station. A thick blanket of winter fog had covered the city and he suddenly realised that he had no idea where he was. At that moment a voice called to him out of the darkness: *'Are you lost, mate?'* Henry replied that he was looking for the station and the stranger kindly offered to show him the way.

As they walked together Henry glanced at his companion and noticed that he was a sergeant in a southern regiment. He noticed, however, that his uniform seemed strangely out of place, more like the uniforms worn at the turn of the century.

111

'Are you going back to your unit?' said the stranger. Henry replied that he was.

'So am I,' said the other man, *'I have to catch a train from here to London.'*

'I too,' said Henry. *'We could travel together, for company, of course.'*

'Sure,' replied the stranger, *'I'll be pleased to have someone to talk to.'*

They soon arrived at the station and boarded the train. They found an empty compartment and settled down for the long journey ahead.

'This night is similar to one night in 1899. I will never forget it,' the other man remarked.

'A long time to remember 1899!' replied Henry.

'I have very good reason to remember it,' said his companion. *'I'll tell you about it. I was pleased with myself that night. I had found an empty compartment and I settled down to doze a little; then a man got in and sat down opposite me looking at me in a shifty way, he looked mean, and ill at ease, but I was tired, I'd done a hard day's work recruiting for the regiment in Newcastle. I felt in my pocket for a cigarette and I accidentally pulled out my wallet and my pay packet which spilled out onto the floor. I picked it up but the other man was watching intently like a dog watches a rabbit. I was almost dropping off to sleep with fatigue when the man leapt up and made a lunge at me, he had a long knife. I grabbed his wrist and deflected the blade of the knife whereupon we both rolled about on the floor.'*

'Did you win the fight?' Henry asked.

'No,' said the stranger. *'Although my attacker was very thin he was stronger than me and as I tried to reach the window communicating cord he pulled me back and plunged the knife into my chest.'*

'But you were lucky? Did you deflect the blade into a less vulnerable spot?' asked Henry.

'No,' replied his companion, *'I was unlucky, he did not miss, he killed me.'*

'He did what?' exclaimed Henry before realising that he was now very much alone.

THE DEATH VAULT OF BRUNDON HALL

Here is an interesting account of a haunting from *The Haunted Homes and Family Traditions of Great Britain* by John Ingham (1897). It was based on extracts taken from the diary of Richard Harris Barham, author of *The Ingoldsbury Legends*.

Barham states that the story is current in the Carter family, of which his first wife was a member, and that it was told to him by Dr Roberts:

'One day, about the year 1785, two lads, one of whom was the uncle of the lady in question, were playing in the large hall of Brundon Hall, a mansion situated on the borders of Suffolk, and at that time the property of the Carters, but which afterwards passed into the possession of the Hurrells. The attention of the boys was suddenly caught

by the opening of a door, usually kept locked, which led to the more ancient part of the landing; and they were more astonished still by the appearance of a strange lady dressed in blue satin, who slowly walked towards the great staircase, stamped three times on a large slab of blue stone which lay at the foot, and then, continuing her walk across the hall, disappeared through a door opposite the one by which she had entered. The boys, more puzzled than frightened, left off playing and ran and told Mrs Carter, the mistress of the house, and the mother of the narrator's (Mr. Roberts's) uncle. She immediately fainted. Subsequently she told her son that the apparition had been frequently seen by other members of the family, and that there was a very dreadful story connected with it which, however, she declined to communicate. Some years afterwards, the house having, I believe, changed hands in the interval, certain repairs were undertaken, in the course of which the entrance to a large vault was discovered, concealed by the stone upon which the lady in blue satin had stamped. On examination two skeletons were found below; a gold bracelet was on the arm of one, and gold spurs were lying near the feet of the other. In addition, a goblet having some dark-coloured sediment at the bottom, supposed to be blood, was found in a recess in the wall, and a considerable quantity of infants' skulls and bones were heaped up in one corner. Lastly, a considerable sum in gold coin was brought to light.'

Further research failed to cast any light on the history of the sinister vault or the reason behind its horrifying contents.

THE HOLE IN THE GROUND

It was 1947 and the Reverend Alfred Byles was vicar of St. Bartholomew's in Yealmpton, South Devon. It was a Saturday afternoon when he spotted a hole in the churchyard.

He wrote of the incident: *'In the middle of the path I saw a hole, of irregular shape, about a yard in width. I thought it was subsidence, and went into the church and told my wife about it. Coming out shortly afterwards, I found that the hole was very much larger, and asked my wife to come out and see it. We both looked into it, and I suggested lowering myself into it. However, it was of uncertain depth, and when I threw in a stone it bumped against stonework, which we could see and which looked like part of a wall.*

My main concern was to prevent an accident to anyone using the path. I therefore went away to get some planks to cover the hole, which measured about three yards across. In the village street, I met Mr Knight, the local builder and undertaker, and asked him to come and see the hole. On arrival there was no sign of a hole. The path and the grass verges were exactly as before, with no sign of disturbance. Mr Knight seemed rather less puzzled than

St. Bartholomew's Church. (Figgis-West)

I expected, and said, "That's all right, Sir"or words to the effect. He never mentioned the incident again.'

So what was it? A timeslip of a past or future event? And one shudders to think as to what would have happened if the Reverend Byles had lowered himself into that dark and forbidding hole?

THE EYE OF THE BEHOLDER

Mrs Violet Nicholls lived in a semi-detached house in Pattingham, South Staffordshire. The house dated from the 1930s and there was no record of any haunting connected with the building or the land upon which it had been built before she took up residence there with her husband.

One night in 1952 Mrs Nicholls woke up to see a young woman in her 20s with long blonde hair, a full complexion, and a full-length yellow dress 'marked at the waist like a half-moon'. She quickly woke her husband who searched the house for the now-vanished stranger. The search failed to find the mysterious lady in yellow and the husband, somewhat angry at being disturbed, returned to bed and was soon asleep again. Mrs Nichols, still shocked by the appearance of the lady, remained awake in the darkness, tense and restless. You can imagine her terror upon seeing the bedroom door suddenly open. The head of the ghostly lady emerged from behind the door, looked around the room briefly and then vanished again!

It was a week later before the phantom lady returned. It was midday and Violet was alone in the house. She glanced out of the kitchen window only to see the same lady in the yellow dress coming up the garden path. The figure passed the kitchen and disappeared.

The figure never appeared again. Or did she? ... six years later Violet found herself living on her own with her five-year-old son. One evening she sent him to bed and followed him up a few minutes later to tuck him in for the night. She found him staring transfixed at the floor. *'Look mum,'* he said as he pointed to a knothole in one of the floorboards. Her eyes were drawn to the hole and to her horror and amazement she saw a pale blue human eye looking back at them! The eye at first appeared to be frightened and then watchful as it stared back at them, unblinking. It sometimes moved from side to side and then up and down, almost as if trying to escape from the hole. It remained like that for some five to ten minutes before fading away. It was never seen again.

It would be interesting to speculate what would have been found if Mrs Nichols had decided to take up the floorboards in her son's room. But perhaps she was wise not to be too curious. Sometimes I have found it is best to leave some things well alone.

THE FOOL ON THE HILL

It was 1967 and the Beatles had given up touring and were busily working on what many still consider their masterpiece – *Sgt. Pepper's Lonely Hearts Club Band*. During a break in recording, Paul McCartney and Alistair Taylor, who worked for the Beatles, were walking one morning on Primrose Hill with Paul's dog Martha. They were watching the sunrise when they realised Martha had gone missing. *'We turned round to go and suddenly there he was standing behind us,'* Alistair recalled. *'He was a middle-aged man, very respectably dressed in a belted raincoat. Nothing in that, you may think, but he'd come up behind us over the bare top of the hill in total silence.'*

Both Alistair and Paul were certain that the man hadn't been there seconds before as they had both been searching the area for Martha. The man had appeared out of nowhere. They exchanged greetings with the man praising the beautiful view from the hill before walking away. Both Paul and Alistair looked back and were shocked to see no sign of the him. *'He'd just disappeared from the top of the hill as if he'd been carried off into thin air! No one could have run to the thin cover of the nearest trees in the time we had turned away from him, and no one could have run over the crest of the hill,'* exclaimed Taylor.

Paul was particularly unnerved by the incident as only moments before the appearance of the man they had both been pondering the existence of God. The two both felt that they had been witness to something special and after finding Martha and sitting down

Paul McCartney. (Figgis-West)

on a seat, Paul said, '*What the hell do you make of that? That's weird. He was here, wasn't he? We did speak to him?*'

Paul went on to write *The Fool on the Hill*, a song about a visionary who was considered a fool by those who didn't understand him. So did the strange incident on Primrose Hill play a part in the inspiration for the song?

THE FLOATING HEAD

Charles I was executed in 1649 after losing the English Civil War. During his incarceration, he had been kept for a time at Carisbrooke Castle on the Isle of Wight. It is claimed that

Charles I.

Charles managed to escape from the castle and was hidden by Royalists in Billingham Manor, near Chillerton. However, his place of concealment – a narrow space behind a sliding panel in the drawing-room – proved so uncomfortable that he decided to return to the castle of his own accord.

In 1928 Sir Shane and Lady Leslie rented the manor and soon became aware of strange sounds such as footsteps and the clank of swords on the stairway. A figure of a man was

The execution of Charles I.

also seen walking through a wall by the maidservants. The Leslies also discovered a coffin-like space hidden in the wall and wondered if this could be the famed hiding place of Charles Stuart.

One morning the strange noises woke Sir Shane and he decided to try and trace their source. The whole household was awoken and accompanied him to the drawing room where a dim light could be seen shining through a crack around the sliding panel. The panel was removed and the intense glow revealed the severed head of Charles I staring out at them with a pitiful expression on his face. The vision then gradually faded from view, leaving the household both shocked and bewildered.

Sir Shane decided to do some research and found that a previous owner had written in a diary about seeing the same phenomenon twice during his time there. On both occasions, an execution had taken place on the island on the day that the head had been seen. Sir Shane then checked to see if an execution had taken place on the day they had witnessed the apparition and discovered that a prisoner had been executed at Newport that very day.

So had the spirit of Charles been drawn back to this world by the distress felt by those about to face death by execution?

CHAPTER FOURTEEN
THE DEVIL AND MAJOR WEIR

Major Thomas Weir was born in 1595 in Kirkton near Carluke in Lanarkshire. His father was the Laird of Kirkton and it was said that his mother, Lady Jean Somerville, was a clairvoyant. Weir made a name for himself as a soldier and served as a lieutenant in Ulster during the Irish Rebellion of 1641. In 1643 he signed the Solemn League and Covenant which was a treaty between the English Parliament and Scotland. It promised to protect the reformed religion in Scotland and to reform the religion in England and Ireland.

In 1650 Weir was appointed commander of the Edinburgh City Guard and soon acquired a reputation for the ill-treatment of prisoners. He would even mock them on their way to the gallows. It was Weir who led the escort of the royalist Marquis of Montrose to his execution after the latter had been defeated at the Battle of Carbisdale in 1650.

Weir lived in Edinburgh's West Bow with his sister Jane. Both were considered staunch Calvinists and Presbyterians. Weir was described as a tall and dark-complexioned man. His stern countenance was enhanced by a dark cloak and he was never seen without a wooden staff which was decorated with carved centaurs. It was noted that he would grasp the wooden stick tightly when preaching. He was particularly admired for the fervour of his commitment to the church and would often hold religious meetings in his house. He would also visit the homes of others to conduct prayer meetings, including those of married women when their husbands were away.

Such was Weir's religious devotion and the eloquence of his preaching that he acquired the nickname of 'Angel Thomas'. It was said of him '*that, [he] could not so much as endure to look upon an Orthodox [Anglican] Minister; but when he met any of them in the street, he would pull his hat over his eyes in a pharisaical kind of indignation and contempt.*'

But all was not as it seemed. The community was shocked when one woman accused Weir of immoral conduct with an animal. No one would believe her story and the woman was tried for slander and publicly whipped after being found guilty. But more was to come. An Edinburgh lady claimed to have had a strange experience when walking past Weir's house with her maid. It was around midnight and the pair were returning home from Castlehill after helping a relative with the birth of her child. As they neared Weir's home, they saw three women by a window. All three were shouting, laughing and applauding. As they passed the front door, they saw the figure of a woman, twice the height of a normal human being. She cackled and writhed before them before vanishing down Anderson's Close. The lady and her maid looked down the alley and saw it flooded with torchlight. The close then echoed with strange laughter and they fled home in terror. The next day the two ladies returned to the area and retraced their steps. The scene of the weird happenings was indeed at Weir's.

It was not long after this that Weir, now in his 70s, fell ill. After his recovery, he attended a prayer meeting where he made a terrible confession. He declared to the shocked congregation to have practised witchcraft, fornication, bestiality, incest and sodomy. To make matters worse, he even claimed to have *'lain with the Devil in the shape of a Beautiful Woman.'* Weir also implicated his sister Jean in his confession.

His claims were at first treated with scepticism and the matter was hushed up for several months. A minister finally brought the matter to the attention of the Lord Provost of Edinburgh, Sir Andrew Ramsay, who had Weir examined by physicians to establish the state of his sanity. It was decided that he was sane and was suffering from a guilty conscience. Thomas and his sister were arrested and the pair were taken to the Edinburgh Tollbooth to await questioning.

Thomas was questioned and readily confirmed his earlier confession. He also admitted to seeing the Devil but *'any fealling he ever hade of him was in the dark, and this is treuth.'*

His sister was then interviewed and her testimony sealed their fate. She admitted that she and her brother had made a pact with the Devil in September 1648. She also spoke of a tall woman with a child on her back and two more at her feet who came to her and offered to barter on her behalf with the Queen of the Fairies. The following day, a small woman visited her and gave her a piece of wood which resembled a root. This object, she was told, would enable her to have the power to do as she wished. The woman then put a cross on the floor and told Jean to place her foot on it. She was then told to place her hand on her head and repeat three times these words: *'All my cross and troubles go to the door with thee.'* Jean then gave the woman some food and all the silver she had. The woman left and Jean found that she could now spin yarn faster than any woman alive. She also claimed that she and her brother had inherited their talent for sorcery from their mother and told of how Thomas bore the mark of the Devil on his right shoulder. Her own mark was in the form of a horseshoe which appeared on her forehead when she frowned. She further revealed that her brother worked his magic through his carved wooden staff and spoke of them roaming the countryside in a fiery coach. It was during one of these

Major Weir's home in Edinburgh.

Major Weir's phantom coach.

trips on 3 September 1651 that a strange man had informed her brother that Oliver Cromwell had defeated the Scottish and Royalist forces at Worcester that very day. She claimed that Weir's staff had been given to him by the Devil and advised her examiners to keep it away from her brother because *'if he chanced to get it into his hands he would certainly drive them all out of doors, notwithstanding all the resistance they could make.'* She then showed them several pieces of old cloth in which a root and money were wrapped.

Her examiners returned to West Bow and found a tavern where they looked at the money. The pieces of cloth were thrown into a fireplace where it was said they circled and danced as they burned. The root was also consigned to the flames. This made strange popping sounds before vanishing up the chimney with a crack like the sound of a small cannon. One of the officials took the money home and put it in a closet. The man's wife heard terrible sounds 'like the falling of a house' coming from the room where the money had been placed. She rushed in but was surprised to find that her husband had heard nothing.

The brother and sister were brought to trial on 9 April 1670. Weir was accused of incest with his sister and his stepdaughter. All mention of witchcraft was dropped as many were embarrassed that such a well-known Presbyterian could have indulged in Satanic practices. He was also accused of bestiality with horses and cattle and adultery with *'several and diverse persons,'* and fornication with Bessie Weems, *'his servant maid, whom he kept in his house. . . for the space of twenty years, during which time he lay with her as familiarly as if she had been his wife.'* Jane was accused of incest and of *'consulting witches, necromancers, and devils'*.

The trial was swift with members of Weir's own family being brought forward to confirm the tales of incest and debauchery.

The court, unsurprisingly, found the pair guilty and they were sentenced to death. Weir and his sister were kept at the leper colony of Greenside until the time of their execution. Thomas was strangled and then burnt to death at Gallow Lee on 11 April 1670. He was offered the chance to repent but refused and replied *'Let me alone. I will not. I have lived as a beast, and must die as a beast.'* His staff were also consigned to the flames. Onlookers claimed that it took an unusual time to burn and twisted strangely in the flames.

Jean was hanged at the Grassmarket the next day. When told of her brother's execution, she spoke of him now being with the devils. She also expressed great anger upon hearing that his staff had been burnt. She also refused to repent and claimed that she intended to die *'with all the shame I can.'* Jean proved good to her promise by striking the executioner and trying to remove her clothes as she was prepared for her death.

Weir's house remained empty for over a century after his death. Rumours of it being haunted ensured that the people of Edinburgh gave it a wide berth. Thomas Stevenson – Robert Louis Stevenson's father – remembered stories of people being disturbed at night by the sounds of the Devil's coach taking Weir and his sister to Dalkeith. The staircase adjoining the house was also cursed and people climbing it would suddenly feel as if they were going downstairs. Jean Weir's apparition, her face blackened by fire, was also seen. Even Weir's old staff was said to haunt the house and the surrounding area. It was claimed that it could be seen dancing about with a lantern hanging from its handle of carved heads.

Around the year 1780, an ex-soldier called William Patullo finally dared to move into the deserted house with his wife. They left the following morning after claiming to have been awakened in the night by a ghostly light in their bedroom. This turned into a calf which placed its front legs on their bed. The apparition stared at them in silence before vanishing.

In 1825 Robert Chambers wrote of the house in his Traditions of Edinburgh:

'His house, though known to be deserted by everything human, was sometimes observed at midnight to be full of lights and heard to emit strange sounds, as of dancing, howling, and, what is strangest of all, spinning. Some people occasionally saw the Major issue from the low close at midnight, mounted on a black horse without a head, and gallop off in a whirlwind of flame.'

The house remained empty for several more decades and was said to have been knocked down in the 1830s. In 2014 it was discovered that parts of Weir's house still existed and now formed part of the Quaker Meeting House in Victoria Terrace. Anthony Buxton, manager of the building, expressed surprise at this revelation but did confirm that one of his staff had seen Major Weir's ghost walk through the wall.

To this day, people are still puzzled by the Weir's confession. Were the pair insane or had they really been leading a double life for decades? From the testimony of family members, it does appear that the brother and sister were guilty of sexual crimes. Were the Weir's tales of witchcraft added to the mix by them in order to further shock the already horrified people of Edinburgh? All we can say for certain is that both met their deaths defiantly and without a shred of remorse.

CHAPTER FIFTEEN
THE GHOSTS OF ST ALBANS

St Albans was founded by the Romans who built a town in the fields below what is the modern city. St Albans takes its name from Alban, a Roman citizen, who protected a Christian priest during a time of persecution. He was so impressed with the priest's piety that he converted to Christianity. He gave himself up in place of the priest and was executed after refusing to renounce his new-found faith. He was taken for execution to a hill above the Roman town and this is where the Saxon abbey and settlement was founded in the eighth century.

I first visited St Albans as a child and quickly became fascinated by its history and wealth of ancient buildings. I also discovered that it could boast a few ghosts!

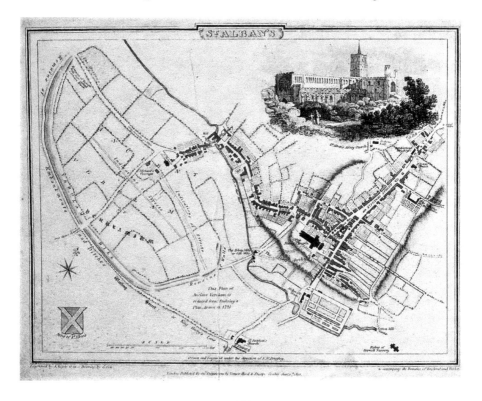

THE ABBEY

St Albans Abbey features a wealth of architecture from the Norman and mediaeval periods and was constructed using material from the abandoned Roman town of Verulamium – the central tower consists almost entirely of Roman tiles. It was heavily restored – or some say over-restored – in the 19th century by Edmund Beckett, the 1st Baron Grimthorpe.

With so much history it is hardly surprising to learn that the building is haunted.

All Souls Day in 1931 saw the assistant verger opening the building for the first services of the day when he encountered several Benedictine monks walking towards him. He stood aside to let them pass, whereupon they vanished into the stonework. A curate saw the same figures several years later.

An unnamed lady heard music coming from the locked abbey one night. She looked through a window and could see just a single candle burning in the darkness. Another woman was passing the abbey one Summer evening when she heard the sounds of choral music coming from inside. She tried to gain entry by the west door but found it locked. As she touched the doorknob the music stopped.

In the early 1930s a man heard singing and saw candlelight coming from the Lady Chapel. It was 2am and the abbey was again locked. He heard it again on several other occasions when passing by the ancient building. Two other people, also in the 1930s, heard organ music the day after Boxing Day. The time was 1.30am. The abbey was locked and empty.

One September evening, a lady saw four tall monks walking along the path from the abbey gateway to the west front. They were described as swaying from side to side like thin trees and appeared to be carrying a coffin. This same witness also saw a monk in a grey habit in the vicinity of the modern chapter house. This same figure has also been seen in the Hudson Memorial Library.

Frances Glossop told of her husband, the Canon George Glossop, hearing music coming from the abbey one night as he worked on a sermon in their home in nearby Romeland. It grew louder and louder and then suddenly faded away. On another occasion, just after the First World War, Glossop heard the organ being played as he walked past the abbey one spring morning. He let himself in through the slype door and walked up to the organ loft. The music stopped as he reached it. There was no one there.

In 1921 a special service was held in the abbey to commemorate the 400th anniversary of the death of Robert Fayrfax, a Tudor composer who is buried in the building. He was Master of the King's Musik and composed a piece in honour of St Alban, the *Albanus Mass*. This music was performed as part of the concert and Glossop recognised it as the music he had heard coming from the locked Abbey as he had composed his sermon.

The South West View of the Abby Church of St Alban

Glossop's daughter also revealed that she had once heard singing outside their Romeland home. She looked out of the window but could see nothing. She called her father and both went outside where they heard invisible singers heading towards the abbey. The singers then seemed to pass through the locked main entrance of the building.

It was the last Christmas Eve of World War Two and Basil Saville, a 16-year-old boy, entered the abbey to fire-watch as part of his air-raid duties. Patrolling the building he started to feel uneasy as he made his way towards the Shrine of St Alban in the Saint's Chapel. Above the shrine was a watching chamber where the monks used to keep an eye on the pilgrims below. Basil thought he could see two cowled figures looking down at him. He called out and climbed the stairway, shining his torch into the darkness. The figures had gone but two discarded monks habits could be seen on the floor.

He made for the Lady Chapel and then climbed the staircase to the roof. As he did so, a bell began to toll in the belfry. He knew this was impossible as all the bells had been taken down for the duration of the war. Basil stood on the roof of the moonlit tower and took in breaths of cold air. He then made his way back down the stairs. The organ began to play and he noticed a candle burning in the organ loft. He called out *Put that light out* and then saw that the organ seat was empty. Despite this, he could see the keys being played and the pages of a music book being turned. He hurried back downstairs and found himself in the choir stalls. The music had now stopped. Looking towards the altar, he saw a procession of monks and an abbot all holding candles. They moved towards the Saint's Chapel and passed through the screen doors which then closed behind them. Basil followed the figures but found the chapel silent and empty. He rushed back upstairs and found the spent candle and music book. The book was black with yellowing pages. He opened it and read the title – it was the *Albanus Mass* by Robert Fayrfax.

Basil then walked to the vestry where he met a fellow fire-watcher who had just arrived. His colleague had seen and heard nothing. The boy explained what had happened and the pair searched the watching chamber and organ loft. The discarded habits and the spent candle had vanished.

Basil went home and immediately wrote down what he had witnessed while his mind was still fresh. He only revealed what he had seen in 1982 when a newspaper, the *Evening Post-Echo,* asked readers for any Christmas ghost stories. He also recounted his experiences to Betty Puttick who wrote of it in her book, *Ghosts of Hertfordshire.*

Incense is often smelt on the south side of the abbey and another ghost, nicknamed Henry, is said to haunt the upper reaches of the building. An 'extra' bishop was once seen standing in the shadows during the enthronement for a new bishop. In the late 1970s, a businessman attended a Remembrance Day service in the abbey. He saw a man dressed in World War Two uniform of an RAF sergeant and discovered that others had also seen the figure there. He is supposed to be the spirit of a local crewman lost in a bomber raid over Germany.

THE GATEHOUSE

The gatehouse was built in 1365. It once housed the monk's printing press and at the Dissolution of the Monasteries became a prison for the next few hundred years. In 1871

The Abbey Gatehouse.

it became part of St Albans School. The sounds of screams – presumably from its time as a prison – have been heard in the building. Windows and doors have also been opened and closed by unseen hands. The sounds of hobnailed boots have been heard in the nearby school building, especially when the old biology department was being demolished. A master heard footsteps on the stairs as he locked the door to the building for the very last time. It is surmised that the sounds are that of a former caretaker who favoured such footwear.

ROMELAND

Romeland Cottage, adjacent to the abbey, is thought to stand on the site of the building's charnel house. In the early part of the 20th century it was occupied by the Skeat family one of whom, Francis, went on to design stained-glass windows, including one for St Peter's Church in St Albans.

Shortly before Francis was born, a Swedish maid, Hilma, was climbing the stairs to bed when she felt a presence. Her candle suddenly went out and she found herself pinned against the wall. She then saw a cowled figure who started to speak to her in a foreign language. The apparition then vanished. The next night she awoke in her room to see the same figure standing at the foot of her bed. The moon was shining through the window and she could see that the ghost was wearing a metal medal around its neck. Canon Glossop was told of this and went to the cottage to speak to the maid. He realised that the 'foreign language' was probably Latin and noted that her description of the medal matched a medal of St Alban which was given to pilgrims upon reaching the abbey. An exorcism was carried out and the figure was never seen again.

YE OLDE FIGHTING COCKS

This pub in Abbey Mill Lane is claimed to be the oldest in all of England. It was originally located nearer to the abbey and was moved here in 1539 after the building was dissolved under Henry VIII. Its octagonal shape is attributed to its former use as a pigeon house. Most of the present structure dates from the 1600s but it is said that the foundation's date from the Saxon period. Tunnels are thought to run between the abbey and the pub's cellars which were once used by monks. Oliver Cromwell is believed to have spent a night at the pub during the English Civil War.

In 2001, at 9.30 in the morning, a member of staff claimed to have witnessed a group of monks in brown habits in the cellar. They were only visible from the knees up. They then climbed the stairs from the cockpit to a fireside table where they promptly vanished.

Ye Olde Fighting Cocks. (Figgis-West)

Another staff member was found shaking with fear after saying that they had seen a ghost. They refused to say what they had witnessed.

The pub landlord also had a brush with the ghosts when he left some keys on the bar as he went into the cellar to change the barrels. When he returned upstairs he saw the keys swinging violently from a key holder. The pub was locked and he was the only person – living that is – in the building.

THE WHITE HART HOTEL

The White Hart Hotel dates from the 1470s and claims to be the most haunted building in St Albans. William Hogarth, the famous artist, came here in 1746 to sketch Lord Lovat, who was being taken to London for trial following the collapse of the Jacobite rebellion in 1745. Lovat had been one of the key supporters of Bonnie Prince Charlie. He was found guilty and executed on Tower Hill the following year.

Room eight is said to be the most haunted in the hotel. Guests have found towels strewn across the bathroom and one guest found writing on the bedroom mirror. It was written in a chalky substance and the writing was described as being 'big and bold' and 'sort of childish'. It said '*Meet me in Room 7 at 8.30*'. The man informed the landlady, Evie Scully, who then rubbed it out. The guest returned to the room only to discover that the writing had returned! A figure has been witnessed sitting at the end of the bed and an indentation, as if someone has been sitting there, has often been noted. I recently stayed in the haunted room and left a packet of sugar on the couch to see what would happen. I left the hotel and returned a couple of hours later. The packet had vanished! No one had entered the locked room in my absence. The receptionist told me that recently she

The White Hart Hotel. (John West)

had received a phone call from room eight. No one was at the end of the line when she answered. This is hardly surprising as the room was empty at the time!

Guests in room seven often smell chicken and a blazing fire was once observed in the blocked-up fireplace.

A little girl has been seen around the hotel, especially on the stairs and near the fireplace in the bar. Her apparition is believed to date from 1803 when a five-year-old child was killed in a fire after being trapped in the cellar. Barrels in the cellar have been thrown about, lights have been turned on and off and a door also locks and unlocks itself. Cold breezes, shadows and the feeling of someone standing behind you are just some of the other strange things experienced in the building.

The attic rooms are supposedly haunted by a prostitute with grey hair. In 2008 a male guest told of feeling icy hands around their neck as they sat on a bed. A chef staying here once dreamt that he was being strangled by a grey-haired woman.

In 1820 a lady called Elizabeth Wilson was travelling by coach to the hotel. She failed to duck as they approached the entrance and she was killed instantly as her head struck the overhead beam. Since then, the figure of a lady in grey has sometimes been seen looking out of the hotel windows. It is surmised that the figure is Elizabeth Wilson.

In 2001 the crew from a TV series, *Ghost Detectives*, visited the White Hart. During filming, a camera in the cellar was found to have had a cable wrenched from it. No one was near the camera at the time. The two mediums involved in the show claimed to have made contact with a Sarah, a Sir William and even William Shakespeare.

ECHOES OF A BATTLE

St Albans has had the misfortune to witness two battles during the War of the Roses – the first battle was fought on 22 May 1455 and the second on 17 February 1461. The origins of the conflict lay in a power struggle between the Dukes of York and Somerset in the vacuum left by King Henry VI, who was suffering from some sort of mental illness. The war dragged on for over 32 years and was to end with the accession of Richard III and his ultimate defeat by Henry Tudor at the Battle of Bosworth.

The first battle here has a strange legend attached to it. Somerset had received a prophecy from Roger Bolingbroke, a soothsayer, who said of the Duke *'Let him shun castles.'*

The battle, which lasted little more than half an hour, was a complete victory for the Yorkist cause. Surprised by a ferocious charge by the Earl of Warwick into the market square, several of Somerset's allies were killed and Henry himself was wounded and captured.

Somerset took refuge in the Castle Inn, on the corner of what is now Chequer Street and Victoria Street – a blue plaque now marks the spot. He then tried to fight his way out but was fatally wounded – right in front of the Castle Inn. The prophecy had been fulfilled.

Battlefield House, a half-timbered Tudor building in Chequer Street, was built near the site of the Lancastrian defence line. The sounds of battle, galloping horses, the clash

St Albans was the scene of two battles in the Wars of the Roses.

of steel and the shouts of men were often heard there. The sound of chanting monks was also heard. A resident of the town remembered staying in the house as a young girl. She describes witnessing a faceless figure wearing a caped greatcoat and beaver hat. The house was demolished in the last century and shops now occupy the spot.

Folly Lane and Catherine Street are also haunted by the sounds of muffled footsteps and drumbeats and Hollywell Hill will sometimes echo to the cries of battle, including the command of 'A-Warwick! A-Warwick!'

Bernards Heath is the site of a possible time slip – part of the Second Battle of St Albans was fought here. Betty Puttick, who we mentioned earlier in this chapter, was walking her dog across the common when she noticed something strange about the trees. They were completely still and appeared like 'a painted backdrop'. As she walked into a wooded area 'all hell broke loose'. She was suddenly surrounded by violent movement. She could feel horses rearing up around her and the sounds of neighing, shouts and the clash of swords filled her ears. She threw her arms over her head to protect herself and rushed to escape. She then noticed a man sitting with his back to a tree. He was wearing a leather cap, jerkin and leggings. He carried a bow and arrows and appeared to be wounded as he was holding his head in his hands as if in pain. The apparition then faded away and all was silent again. Betty's dog came running towards her and the two quickly made for home. Betty often returned to Bernards Heath but was never again to experience what she believed was a brief return to a battle fought so long ago.

VERULAMIUM PARK

The town of Verulamium was one of the finest in all of Roman Britain. The remains of defensive walls, a theatre, a mosaic floor in situ and a rich collection of artefacts in the site museum all testify to its past greatness. With over 400 years of Roman occupation, it is hardly surprising that some of the ghosts of its former inhabitants are said to haunt the area.

In 1985 a man in his 20s was walking through the park one night. He was shocked to see a Roman centurion on a horse suddenly appear before him. He was so scared that he fled from the scene, falling and injuring his shoulder and knee in the process. He ended up being treated in a local hospital.

John 'Ginger' Mills, a former circus performer, lived for many years in a camper van by the lake in the park. Early one morning he was walking around the park when he heard the sounds of marching feet behind him. He stood aside and felt an icy breeze as the unseen figures went by.

Verulamium Park. (Figgis-West)

A ghost from a much later date also haunts the park. His only recorded appearance was in 1970. It was the Christmas period and two boys were cycling through the park one misty evening when they saw a figure in a silvery haze gliding towards them. He had long, curly hair and was carrying a sword. He was wearing a tunic with silver buttons and tassels, baggy trousers and high boots. He was seen by the boys to glide towards the bridge.

The park's most puzzling apparition appeared one Easter morning in 2004. A rust-coloured tornado, the size of a man, suddenly appeared before a group of startled walkers. It was described as 'an amazing mass of swirling energy' which hovered in front of the witnesses before suddenly jumping into the stream. The 'tornado' then sank into the water but a whirlpool, larger than a dinner plate, appeared at its vanishing point. This was seen to travel towards the bridge next to the Ye Olde Fighting Cocks.

King Harry Lane is the site of a Roman cemetery. Archaeologists excavating the site became aware of a 'presence' during the dig. Romans have also been seen in Kingsbury Avenue and Camlet Way.

Camp Road, especially the area in the vicinity of the former Camp pub, is haunted by the sounds of marching feet on gravel. It is assumed that these sounds are the last psychic traces of Roman soldiers who were stationed hereabouts.

The ruins of old Gorhambury House, an Elizabethan mansion, is said to be the home of several ghostly Roman soldiers.

One November night, a group of people were driving from Wheathampstead to their homes in St Albans. The driver suddenly saw and heard a column of marching Roman

St Peter's Church. (Figgis-West)

soldiers. An impressive standard-bearer was at their head. Strangely, the passengers did not see the figures but did hear the marching feet and the sounds of jangling armour.

ST PETER'S CHURCH

The oldest ghost story in St Albans dates from 1258. A hermit was sitting in the churchyard when he saw a bearded man rush past him and climb the church tower. He was then heard to call out, *'Woe! Woe! To all the inhabitants of the Earth.'* It was not long after this vision that a great famine and pestilence hit England. In London alone it is said that over 15,000 people died.

THE CROWN AND ANCHOR

This former pub stands on the corner of Sopwell Lane. It dates from the 15th century and was first used as a hostel for visitors to the abbey. The building is now a private residence but several years ago was the office of an estate agent called Strutt and Parker. Leo Hickish, a partner in the business, was coming into work one day when a scared colleague pointed to some wet footprints on the stone floor at the bottom of the stairs. The footprints were of someone walking around barefoot. No one else was in the building and neither could explain how the footprints had got there.

In the late 1990s, one of the estate agents saw the gaunt face of a young woman appear between filing cabinets in an upstairs office. It was seen near a window where a 14th-century gallery once stood. Staff also reported feeling uneasy in the upstairs rooms and lights were turned on and off when no one was near them. Pipe tobacco was also smelt and this was attributed to the ghost of an English Civil War Cavalier who sits beside a downstairs fireplace. In the 1980s a monk was also seen standing beside a fireplace in the adjoining building. This separate dwelling originally formed part of the pub.

The former Crown and Anchor pub. (Figgis-West)

A group of paranormal investigators visited the building. They used dowsing rods which appeared to indicate that several ley lines crossed the area. Marion Goodfellow, the team's medium, sensed a man in the cellar who was wearing an apron. In an upstairs room, she picked up the impression of a woman near to where the estate agent had seen the gaunt face. The medium also sensed a man who was short of breath. He had apparently died in the building from a heart condition. Pipe tobacco was also smelt.

DONNINGTON HOUSE

Donnington House in St Peter's Street was the scene of much excitement one Sunday evening in 1872 when 200 people gathered outside to catch sight of a ghost in a white hat which had been seen at an upstairs window. The police were called and a search was made of the house but no one was found. Despite this, one elderly lady in the crowd claimed to have seen 'something' in the house and others said they had heard tapping sounds at a window. Another claimed to have heard the 'ghost' speak but what the apparition said was sadly not recorded.

It is thought that the ghost – if indeed it was a ghost – was the butler of Dr William Alexander Russell, a surgeon and former resident of the house who had died in 1869. The butler had been caught stealing brandy and was dismissed in disgrace. Filled with remorse, the man killed himself in an upper room. The butler wore a white wig and the witness may have mistaken it for a white hat.

The building was later renamed Mallinson House and is now the home for the National Pharmacy Association. Members of staff have found that stationary has been moved or vanished without a trace. In 1977 a builder was working late one evening when he saw the figure of a man walk past him and ascend the stairs. The phantom had no legs. Technicians working at the Abbey Theatre often saw a solitary light shining out from a middle upstairs window when passing the deserted building in the middle of the night.

CHAPTER SIXTEEN
SCOTTISH TALES OF TERROR

THE MURDERESS OF KILLIECRANKIE

Elliott O'Donnell was one of the foremost paranormal investigators of the last century. He published numerous books on ghosts and many of these feature tales from north of the border. One such story was told to him by a lady who was on a cycle tour of Scotland. It concerns the Pass of Killiecrankie, the scene of a terrible 17th century battle which took place between the Jacobites and troops loyal to William of Orange.

The year was 1909 and O'Donnell's informant had made her base in Pitlochry. She decided to visit the Pass of Killicrankie late one evening and had perched herself on a rock at the foot of one of the cliffs. She became lost in thought as she surveyed the beauty of the place and did not notice that it was getting late. Coming out of her daydream, she suddenly realised that it was getting dark. As she had a warm cape and plenty of food she decided to camp out in the pass until morning. She picked a suitable boulder and climbed on top of it. She soon fell asleep but was awakened at 2am by a dull boom which sounded to her like distant musket fire.

She became aware of growing dread and the realisation that she was totally alone. The screech of an owl broke the silence and she laughed nervously, trying to take her mind from the fear by tightening her skirt and tying knots in her shoelaces. The sudden crack of musket fire then sounded around her and from nowhere came the running, panting figure of a Highlander. His face was filled with fear as if all the demons of Hell were chasing him. His long hair was blowing in the wind and she noticed how his skin was without any colour. His dress consisted of a kilt, coat, sporran, empty scabbard and shoes. She saw that one of the buckles on his shoes was missing and that blood was running down his thighs. As he ran, the sound of scattering gravel accompanied him and yet the smooth road was devoid of any such material. He continued running along the road and darted past her, leaping over rocks and finally vanishing behind some boulders. The sounds of drums, voices and flutes now filled the air. From the furthest end of the Pass a large number of

The Battle of Killiecrankie.

tall soldiers in scarlet uniforms of the 17th century, led by a mounted officer, suddenly appeared. The woman later told O'Donnell how she was struck by their livid eyes and the whiteness of their skin. She became terrified at the thought of them seeing her but was relieved to note that none of them even glanced in her direction as they marched by. They soon vanished from view and she quickly remounted the boulder. It was now 2.30 and she decided to ease her hunger by eating some of the sandwiches. It was at this point that she became disturbed by a rustling sound from a nearby ash tree. It was not windy and yet the tree swayed violently from side to side. To make matters worse, the sounds of groaning appeared to come from the very tree itself.

The woman decided to investigate this strange phenomenon and called on every ounce of her courage as she moved forward to get a closer view of the tree. As she did so, she kicked something and glanced down. The body of an English soldier lay before her, his chest covered in blood from a terrible wound. She looked around and saw dozens of other bodies – English and Highlander – strewn across the grass. One English officer had half his face blown away and she was sickened to see that he was still writhing in pain. Wounded and dead horses were also visible and the smell of blood and the groans of the dying only added to the horror.

As she surveyed the scene, the figure of a beautiful Highland woman suddenly dropped from the tree and began to move about the bodies. She was carrying a wicker basket and knife. Her face took on the look of avarice as she examined the clothing of the English soldiers. She made her way to one wounded English officer and snatched his sword and pistol. She then knelt down and gleefully stabbed him in the heart, moving it back and forth to ensure that he was dead. She then stripped his body of his rings, epaulettes, buttons and gold lace. She moved on to other dying soldiers, hitting them with the butt-ends of their guns or cutting their throats before removing their valuables. In some cases, the rings proved too stubborn to remove and she cut off their fingers. These were then placed in the basket alongside her other spoils of war. She had murdered ten soldiers in all when she suddenly glanced up and became aware of being watched by the woman from the 20th century. She immediately screamed in rage and rushed towards her. The Highlander raised her knife and was about to strike when her intended victim collapsed in fear and passed out.

It was morning before O'Donnell's informant recovered. The bodies of the soldiers and the murderous woman had vanished. The woman fled the Pass and vowed never again to return to that place of death.

THE NIGHT OF TERROR

Shirley Brown was a student nurse at Dundee Hospital. She had arrived in the town in the autumn of 1974 and after some six months had been able to rent a small flat in a tenement building in Morgan Street with a fellow student nurse called Gail Bruce.

One morning in January 1976 Shirley woke up to find Gail looking strangely at her. She asked if Shirley was feeling well and then said she would elaborate further at lunchtime. During their meal Gail explained that she had trouble sleeping and was still awake at 3.30am when the hall light came on. Just after this, the sounds of slow, padding footsteps could be heard coming from the bathroom. She was naturally terrified but was somewhat reassured as their bedroom door was locked.

Gail decided to hide under the bedclothes but then, after a few minutes, to look out from under the covers. The hall light was now switched off. She looked around and was shocked to see an elderly woman with short grey hair and a light blue nightgown or dress standing by her friend's bed!

The two were talking but Gail could not hear what they were saying. She was suddenly filled with a sense of evil and she closed her eyes. When she opened them she found that the woman had vanished.

It is hardly surprising to learn that both ladies were now very frightened and vowed never again to be in the flat alone. A week passed with no new occurrences and both women began to relax again. One night Shirley was in bed reading while Gail finished in the bathroom. It was now just before midnight and Shirley suddenly realised that someone was moving about in the kitchen. She decided to tap on the wall which separated the bedroom from the kitchen to see if Gail had gone in there unnoticed.

In response to her tap Shirley was terrified to hear the sounds of something which appeared to be trying to claw its way through the walls to get to her. She called out and Gail, who was still in the bathroom, rushed out. It was at this point that the sounds stopped. The two women sat on the bed together only to hear the terrifying sounds start up again. This time the clawing sounds were even more savage. It seemed as if the thing – whatever it was – was determined to claw its way through the wall to reach them. The terrible sounds continued for over a quarter of an hour before the pair finally decided to get dressed and flee the flat. They suddenly realised to their horror that the keys to the front door were in the living room where the thing now was. They bravely decided to risk facing it and rushed into the living room. They turned on the light and the room was instantly filled with a blue flash as the bulb fused. The two groped their way in the darkness but managed to find the keys before dashing to a friend's flat.

The two friends decided to vacate their home. They returned during the day to collect their possessions and look at the spot where the thing had tried to claw through the wall. There was not even the sign of a scratch. They were tempted to look into the history of the flat to find out what could be behind their frightening experience but finally decided against it. They were simply too scared in case they discovered something even more terrifying than their ordeal of the night before.

THE DEATH BOGLE

Elliot O'Donnell himself had a strange experience during a stay in Scotland. He was lodging in Pitlochry and decided to take a break from his writing by spending the day at Loch Tay. He finally made for home at 7pm, cycling back along a deserted moonlit road. He paused at the junction of four roads, a mile or two from Pitlochry, and decided to rest by a sign-post. He stood there for some ten minutes and was about to remount his bicycle when he suddenly became icy cold. He was filled with an inexplicable terror and let the bicycle fall to the ground. He was then shocked to see something appear with a thud on an open space before him. It was standing bolt upright and was described by O'Donnell as being like a 'blurred and indefinite cylindrical pillar'.

O'Donnell then heard the sound of rumbling wheels and a wagon carrying hay rolled into view. A man in a wide-brimmed straw hat and a boy in corduroys were sitting at the front. The horse suddenly caught sight of the glowing figure in the road and started to

Elliott O'Donnell.

snort in fear. The man cried out, *'Hey! Hey! What's the matter with ye, beast?'* He then saw the thing before them. *'Great God! What's yon figure that I see? What's yon figure, Tammas?'*

The boy grabbed the man's hand and screamed, *'I dinna ken, I dinna ken, Matthew, but take heed, mon, it does not touch me. It's me its come after, na ye.'*

The horse now sped forward and dashed past the phantom. The boy was nearly thrown into the road but managed to stay on the wagon as the thing bounded after them with long spidery arms. O'Donnell did not wait to see if it caught them but grabbed his bicycle and raced back to his lodgings as if his very life depended on it ... which perhaps it did.

He explained what had happened to his landlady who suddenly became very serious. She told him that spot in the road was long known to be haunted.

'It was stupid of me not to warn you ... None of the peasants round here will venture within a mile of it after twilight, so the carters you saw must have been strangers. No one has ever seen the ghost except in the misty form in which it appeared to you. It does not frequent the place every night, it only appears periodically, and its method never varies. It leaps over a wall or hedge, remains stationary till someone approaches, and then pursues them with monstrous springs. The person it touches invariably dies within a year. I well recollect when I was in my teens, on just such a night as this, driving home with my father from Lady Colin Ferner's croquet party at Blair Atholl. When we got to the spot you name, the horse shied, and before I could realise what had happened, we were racing home at a terrific pace. My father and I sat in front, and the groom, a Highland boy from the valley of Ben-y-gloe, behind. Never having seen my father frightened, his agitation now alarmed me horribly, and the more so as my instinct told me it was caused by something other than the mere bolting of the horse. I was soon enlightened. A gigantic figure, with leaps and bounds, suddenly overtook us, and, thrusting out its long, thin arms, touched my father lightly on the hand, and then with a harsh cry, more like that of some strange animal than that of a human being, disappeared. Neither of us spoke till we reached home – I did not live here then, but in a house on the other side of Pitlochry – when my father, who was still white as a sheet, took me aside and whispered, "Whatever you do, Flora, don't breath a word of what has happened to your mother, and never let her go along that road at night. It was the death bogle. I shall die within twelve months." And he did.

I cannot describe the thing any more than you can, except that it gave me the impression it had no eyes. But what it was, whether the ghost of a man, woman or some peculiar beast, I could not, for the life of me, tell.'

THE CALL OF IONA

Iona is said to contain the tombs of some 60 kings and was the site of a monastery founded by Saint Columba. It is hardly surprising to learn that ghostly monks in brown robes haunt the island. They never speak or make a sound and are often accompanied by blue, twinkling lights. It is said that the monks first appeared after the Reformation when many of the grave markers from the monk's cemetery were cast into the sea.

The south side of the island has a sinister reputation. Elementals are said to haunt the area and strange music has been heard there.

Iona is also the location of a time slip. Peter Underwood was told of an artist called John MacMillan who was out walking one midsummer evening along the road from the abbey towards White Sands. He decided to visit a friend who lived in a croft but suddenly realised that he could not see it. The croft of another friend had also vanished. He carried on walking towards White Sands and noticed how the landscape had changed. None of the familiar landmarks were there.

As he neared White Sands, he saw a fleet of Viking ships appear from behind an islet known as Eilean Annraidh. There were 14 ships in all and he could see the emblems on the sails and the men who appeared to be shouting as they neared the shore. A group of monks were watching them. The Vikings jumped down from the boats and murdered the monks before they had time to flee. He then saw the Vikings make for the abbey. No sound accompanied his vision and all sense of time was lost. The Vikings finally reappeared with cattle and loot from the abbey which had been set on fire. The Vikings loaded up their booty and sailed off into the darkness.

The artist sketched the emblems seen on the sails of the longboats. He approached someone at the British Museum who confirmed the designs as belonging to the late tenth century.

Others have also witnessed the Viking longships at White Sands. F. C. B. Cadell, the Edinburgh artist, saw them as did a party of three visitors who assumed that they were watching a rehearsal for a film or historical pageant.

Underwood was also told of three strange occurrences by a former RAF officer called Tommy Frankland. He was visiting the abbey grounds and had climbed some wooden

Tombs of the Kings, Iona Cathedral   Valentines Series

steps. He was half-way up when he encountered a force which prevented him from proceeding. He had no choice but to retrace his steps.

One another occasion, Frankland was walking with two nuns. They were heading for the Bishop's House and had stopped on a headland that separates Larachan Bay from the Bay of Coracles. They looked back towards Larachan and saw three columns of smoke. They were some 20ft in height and appeared to originate from a deserted area. None of them could ever find an explanation for what had caused this.

Frankland also spoke of being in the Bishop's House library one evening with several students. They saw an elderly clergyman by an open window. He was standing still and looking out towards the Sound of Iona. He then left the room and began walking towards the sea. They were shocked to see him walk into the water. He was waist-deep before Frankland reached the shoreline and shouted at him to turn back. The clergy appeared released from his spell and returned to the shore. He explained that he had seen the abbey as it had appeared some 1,000 years ago and thought he was walking along a causeway which led to it. He had been unaware that he was in the sea until he had heard the cries of alarm from behind him.

Alasdair Alpin MacGregor wrote of Iona in *The Ghost Book*. He tells of how one night in 1948 John Moffat, an ex-army physical trainer, was bell ringing in the Abbey Tower. The man described a 'mighty force' which tried to strangle him as he attempted to leave the tower.

Iona is also known for its 'Call'. In August or September 1929 an Italian lady called Marie Emily Fornario – known as Netta to her friends – arrived on the island. She found accommodation with a Mrs MacRae who lived in Traymore. She was soon on friendly terms with her landlady and explained that she had been born in Cairo in 1897. Her father was an Italian doctor and her mother was from England. Her mother had died the year after her birth and her maternal grandfather in London had brought her up after her father decided to return to Italy. She had never been happy as a child as her impatience had often irritated her guardian. She expressed great anger at her father for marrying an Englishwoman as she felt that the offspring of such marriages were doomed to fail in life.

She explained that she had answered the 'Call' of the island as it provided the peace and tranquillity that she yearned for.

Marie was deeply interested in the paranormal and had written articles and reviews for publications such as the *Occult Review* under the name of Mac Tyler. She was also a member of the Alpha et Omega Temple which was the successor organisation of the Hermetic Order of the Golden Dawn, a society dedicated to the study of the occult and spiritual development. She was also suspected of being a member of the Rosicrucian Order, another spiritual group, which had been founded by H. Spencer Lewis in 1915.

Mrs MacRae noted that her lodger was not in the best of health and initially was only able to walk for short distances along a nearby beach. Sometimes she stayed in her room for days on end and wrote poetry. She also studied the folklore of Iona and spoke of having visions and communication with the spirit world. One such vision involved her seeing a rudderless boat sailing across the sky. It was noted by her landlady that Marie's silver jewellery had turned black. She sought an explanation for this and was told by Marie that always happened to her jewellery after wearing it.

Marie continued to explore the island and spent one night lost on the moor after searching for pre-Christian ruins. She further alarmed her landlady by informing her that once she had gone into a trance for a week or more and that Mrs MacRae was not to seek medical aid if it happened to her on the island.

Marie's attitude changed on 17 November. It was Sunday morning and a strange look developed in her eyes. She explained that she must leave the island immediately and return to London. She claimed that certain unnamed people were trying to attack her through telepathic means. She packed all her possessions but was forced to wait as the ferry service would not resume for another day. She retired to her room for several hours but then emerged saying that she was now staying on the island. Her face bore a look of resignation rather than distress and Mrs MacRae helped unpack her belongings. They chatted for some time and then Marie retired to her bed.

The next morning saw Mrs MacRae knock on Marie's door. There was no answer. She opened the door and found that Marie was nowhere to be seen. All her belongings were still there. Several hours went by and there was still no sign of her lodger. Mrs MacRae became alarmed and a search was made of the island. It was two days before two local men found her lying dead by a fairy mound. She was naked. However, some reports claim that she was covered in a black cloak. A silver chain around her neck had turned black and a knife lay nearby. One of her hands rested under her head and a cross was found cut into the turf beneath her. There were scratches on her toes but no other marks on her body. It was obvious that she had been engaged in some magical ritual.

One newspaper – *The Scotsman* – published a report on 27 November which quoted Mrs Varney, her housekeeper in Kew, as saying that Marie did not believe in doctors and would heal people by telepathy. She went on to say, *'If people would let her heal them she would moan and cry piteously, but she was otherwise cheerful and happy. Once she announced her intention to fast for 40 days, but was persuaded to give it up after a fortnight. She dressed in a long cape-like garment made by herself, and never wore a hat. Several times she said she had been to the 'far beyond' and had come back to life after spending some time in another world.'*

It also emerged that a few days before Marie had vanished she had sent a letter to Mrs Varney which read, '*Do not be surprised if you do not hear from me for a long time. I have a terrible case of healing on.*' A search of her room on Iona revealed 'letters of a strange character' which were given to the police.

An inquest was held and it was ruled that she had died of heart failure brought on by exposure. However, many questions remained unanswered. Why had it taken two days to find her on such a small island? Where were her missing clothes and shoes? It was suggested that she may have left the house naked. If that was the case, then why were only her toes injured? The scratches and cuts on her toes appeared to indicate she had been running. But running from what? There were also stories of a cloaked man being seen in the area and blue lights hovering over where the body had been found. The man, if he existed, was never traced.

It is also interesting to note that her father was reported as having a strange sense of foreboding on 17 November. He could not shake off the feeling that something was wrong with his daughter.

Dion Fortune, the occultist and author, said she had known Marie very well. They had often worked together but had finally gone their separate ways. She went on to say that her former colleague had been very interested in Green Ray Elementals (fairies). Fortune felt that she was moving into areas that could prove dangerous. She was convinced that Marie had been astral projecting (a state where a person's life force leaves the body). Fortune suggested that she may have been the victim of a psychic attack. Or had the cold killed Marie's body and prevented her soul from returning to it?

It has also been suggested that Marie was familiar with the work of Fiona MacLeod – the pen name of William Sharp – who wrote of a girl called Elsie whose mother had told Sharp that her daughter was in contact with the ghostly monks of Iona. The monks were hostile to Elsie and she now only felt safe on one spot on the island because of this. The 'safe' area was known as Staonaig where it was said that the monks had burnt a woman to death. According to legend, the monks did not realise that she was a fairy and her death had brought ill-luck to them. Was it a coincidence that Marie was found in the same area? Was she attempting to perform a ritual to bring peace to the fairy woman or seek healing for the monks who had murdered her?

Marie was buried on Iona in the graveyard of St Oran's Chapel. Her simple gravestone, etched with the letters M.E.F. remains there to this day. Her ghost is still said to walk the island.

Tay Bridge before the disaster.

THE TAY BRIDGE DISASTER

The 28 December 1879 was long remembered by our Victorian ancestors as the date when the Tay Bridge in Scotland collapsed during a terrible storm. Unfortunately, a train was travelling across the railway bridge at the time and all 75 passengers and crew perished. Several of the bodies were never recovered.

The Tay Bridge collapses.

The Tay Bridge Disaster shocked Victorian Britain.

It was later found that poor construction and a failure to take into account the pressure of high winds on the structure had made the disaster inevitable.

The wrecked train was salvaged from the river bed, repaired and finally returned to service. Sardonically nicknamed *The Diver*, many engine crews regarded the train as jinxed and refused to take it out. It was finally scrapped in 1919.

Construction work on a new bridge started in 1883 and within four years trains were once again crossing the Tay. The stumps of the original bridge piers can still be seen running alongside the later structure.

Locals still maintain that on the anniversary of the disaster, a phantom train can be seen crossing the bridge at 7.15pm from the Edinburgh side. Its rear red light shines briefly in the darkness before vanishing as the train re-enacts its fatal plunge. Screams are also heard as the engine and its six carriages sink into the waters below.

It was also believed that the ghosts of passengers lost in the disaster would occasionally appear on trains crossing the bridge. One young man joined the train in Fife and found a compartment empty, except for an elderly man dressed in old-fashioned looking clothes. When the train started crossing the Tay Bridge, the old man's features began to contort in fear and horror. He then faded away, leaving the young man alone, confused and very frightened.

CHAPTER SEVENTEEN
CATCH ME WHEN YOU CAN: ROBERT JAMES LEES AND THE HUNT FOR JACK THE RIPPER

Robert James Lees was one of the most respected mediums of the 19th century. He was the author of several books on spiritualism and is said to have held séances for Queen Victoria after the death of her beloved Albert. But it is his connection with Jack the Ripper that still fascinates and intrigues people today.

It is asserted in several books and articles on Jack the Ripper that Lees not only saw the killer in psychic visions but also led Scotland Yard to his very door. So did Lees really solve the most notorious series of murders in the history of crime?

Robert Lees was born in Birmingham in 1849. He grew up in Hinckley, Leicestershire and had his first psychic experience when he was just three-years-old. As he later recalled:

'I am personally aware that as a child I cried at being left in the darkness unless I saw a mysterious and to others invisible kilted Highlander who remained beside me talking or singing till I fell asleep.'

After seeing the apparition, Lees was never afraid of the dark again. At the age of seven, Lees moved with his family to a larger house that was reputed to be haunted. One night, Lees sat up with his father to watch for the ghost. It was around 1am when Robert suddenly went white and collapsed. He was quickly put to bed and woke up

The Ripper flees from the scene of another murder.

THE·WHITECHAPEL MONSTER SEEN BY TWO MEN.

some three hours later. He revealed that he had seen the apparition of a boy walk down the stairs. The figure had lifted its head as it reached the fourth step from the bottom – blood was pouring from its throat. The ghost was seen again the next night. Robert saw it continue down the steps, cross the kitchen and vanish behind the cellar door. The cellar floor was dug up and the skeleton of a boy aged about eight was unearthed. The local police looked at their records and found that a couple had lived in the house with a young boy. They claimed that the boy had gone missing. He was never found and the couple moved to America.

Lees' parents became interested in spiritualism and allowed Robert to take part in a table-turning session where he became sleepy and then fell into a deep sleep. Upon walking up, he was surprised to learn that he had told his parents about being the reincarnation of their first son who had died when he was only 12 hours old.

The family's bible class leader, Aaron Franklin, was told about Robert's apparent mediumistic abilities and decided to attend the next session. He saw the boy go into a trance and contacted *The Spiritual Magazine* who decided to send their editor to the next session. This time Robert went into a trance and was taken over by Prince Albert, Queen Victoria's late husband. The magazine printed an account of the séance and sent a copy to the Queen.

According to the later recollections of Robert's daughter, Eva Lees, Franklin and the editor of the magazine attended another séance with two strangers. After going into a trance, Robert greeted them by name and said he knew why they were there. They then admitted they were there by royal command to see if he had really contacted Prince Albert. They asked for Robert to write a message and sign it with a pet name used by Albert and the individual that he wished to contact – at no time was Victoria's name mentioned by the two men.

The message came through and was written down and sealed. Robert then shook hands with the two men using a masonic sign to prove that they and Albert were members of the same masonic lodge.

It was not long before Lees received a request from Victoria to hold a séance at Windsor. Albert again came through and the Queen was satisfied enough to want to appoint the 14-year-old as her resident medium. During another séance, Robert's spirit guide said that he had other work to do but explained that a boy at Balmoral named John Brown could provide a psychic link for Victoria to contact her husband. Robert should only be sent for in exceptional circumstances, such as if the spirit of Prince Albert was unable to connect with John Brown.

Eva Lees later recalled, 'When we saw a carriage and pair and the two gentlemen occasionally arrive, we knew where he was going and what he was going for but nothing was ever said about the matter outside the family until after his death.'

Lees continued with his spiritualism and pursued a career as a journalist, first writing for the *Manchester Guardian* and then various publications in Fleet Street, including *Tit-Bits* magazine. He also befriended W.T Stead, the noted editor and founder of the spiritualist quarterly *Borderland*.

The autumn of 1888 saw a series of terrible and shocking murders carried out in the East End of London. Five women were brutally slain over a period of several weeks, the last victim being killed on 9 November. Letters claiming to be from the killer were sent to the press. One even included a piece of kidney said to have been taken from one of the women. One sent to the Central News Agency bore the name Jack the Ripper and so a legend was born. No one was tried for the crimes and to this day his identity remains a mystery. Or does it?

On 28 April 1895 the Chicago *Sunday Times-Herald* published a sensational story. It was claimed that Dr Howard, a well-known London physician, had been one of a dozen doctors who had sat in judgement on a fellow physician of high standing. The man in question was Jack the Ripper! A drunken Dr Howard had apparently told the story to William Greer Harrison of the Bohemian Club in San Francisco.

Here is a summary of what was published:

It was claimed that Lees had a vision during the period of the first three murders. He had been working in his study when he saw a blue-eyed man in a dark Scotch tweed suit carrying a light overcoat over his arm. He was walking with a woman down a shabby-looking street. They entered a courtyard where Lees saw a nameplate on the wall and a clock through the lighted window of a nearby gin house. The time on the clock read 12.40am. The woman was clearly drunk and could offer no resistance as the man covered her mouth with his hand and cut her throat with a knife. He then proceeded to mutilate her before wiping the knife on the woman's clothing, then he put on his overcoat to hide the bloodstains on his shirt-front and left the area.

Lees went to Scotland Yard and told detectives about what he had seen. They appeared uninterested but the sergeant on duty did make a note of the time and name of the place as seen in Lees' vision. The very next night a woman was killed in the spot named by Lees. The time of her murder also matched the time seen in the vision. Witnesses had described her as being with a man wearing a dark suit and soft felt hat. He was carrying a coat on his arm and was said to 'look like a gentleman'.

Lees learned of the murder and visited the site with a trusted man-servant. It so shocked his system that he decided to travel to the continent with his family after following advice from his doctor.

After leaving England Lees found that he was no longer troubled by the visions. During his absence the Ripper carried out four more murders.

Lees eventually returned to London and found himself travelling with his wife in an omnibus from Shepherd's Bush. He suddenly became aware of the same sensations that he had experienced in his study. The omnibus climbed Notting Hill and stopped at the top to allow a man on board. Lees looked at the man and noticed that he was of medium size. He was wearing a dark suit of Scotch tweed, a light overcoat and a soft felt hat.

It had been a year since his last vision but he was certain that this man was Jack the Ripper. He told his wife but she laughed it off and said not to be so foolish. Lees was not to be put off and decided to follow the man when he alighted at Marble Arch. Leaving his wife, he followed him down Park Lane. Lees saw a policeman and pointed out the man in the overcoat as Jack the Ripper. The policeman was less than impressed and threatened to run Lees in. It then appeared that the man became aware he was being followed and jumped into a cab upon reaching Apsley House.

Lees found a police sergeant and repeated his suspicions regarding the man in the cab who exclaimed, *'Show me the constable who refused to arrest him! Why it was only this morning that we received news at the Bow Street station that the 'ripper' was coming in this direction.'*

The Illustrated Police News covered the Ripper murders extensively.

Lees received another vision that night – the Ripper was going to kill again. He saw the woman's face and noted that one of her ears was severed. The other was hanging by a shred of skin.

Lees went to Scotland Yard where he demanded a meeting with the head inspector of police. The inspector listened with a smile until he was told of the victim's ears. He then showed Lees a postcard which was written in red ink and bore two bloody finger marks:

Tomorrow night I shall again take my revenge, claiming from a class of women who have made themselves most obnoxious to me my ninth victim.

JACK THE RIPPER

PS. To prove that I am really 'Jack the Ripper' I will cut off the ears of this ninth victim.

The inspector, a religious man, regarded Lees' vision as a sign from God and flooded London with thousands of extra police in plain clothes to prevent the next outrage.

Despite this, the Ripper struck again. The inspector was informed that the victim's ear had been mutilated in the manner described by Lees. The medium was so affected by the latest murder that he left again for the continent. During this time, the Ripper brought his list of victims up to 16, vowing to kill another four and then stop.

Newspaper coverage from 1931 claimed that Lees had helped track down Jack the Ripper.

Lees finally returned to London where he made the acquaintance of two Americans, Roland B. Shaw, a mining stockbroker, and Fred C. Beckwith, a financial promoter of an American syndicate in London.

The three were dining in the Criterion when Lees had another vision, *'Great God! Jack the Ripper has committed another murder.'*

Shaw looked at his watch and noted that it was 7.49pm. Within 20 minutes of Lees' vision, a policeman came across another Ripper victim in Crown Court, Whitechapel.

Lees and his two friends rushed to Scotland Yard and told the inspector of this latest crime. As he did so, a telegram arrived informing the inspector of yet another Ripper murder. The inspector, along with two plain-clothed officers, took the three men to Crown Court where Lees sensed a message written on the wall. The inspector struck a match and immediately saw some words written in chalk. They read *'Seventeen, Jack the Ripper.'*

The Ripper had now been terrorising London for years and the inspector begged Lees to track down the killer. The medium agreed and that very night set out to end the Ripper's reign of terror. Lees sensed the man's energy and led the inspector and his colleagues through the streets of Whitechapel. He finally halted by the gates of a West End mansion. The time was 4 am. He pointed to a lit upper room and said, *'There is the murderer – the man you are looking for.'*

The inspector was astonished. *'It is impossible. That is the residence of one of the most celebrated physicians in the West End.'*

The policeman then asked Lees to describe the interior of the house. The psychic did so in some detail, even mentioning a large mastiff which was sleeping at the bottom of the stairs. They waited until 7am, the time the servants would get up, and then knocked on the door. They were allowed in and discovered that the doctor was still in bed. The interior of the house matched exactly the description given by Lees. Only the dog was missing. One of the servants then confirmed that the dog did sleep at the bottom of the stairs but had been let out into the back garden that morning.

The inspector was convinced. He interviewed the doctor's wife who stated that she believed her husband to be of unsound mind. He had threatened her and their children and she had been forced to lock herself up to avoid him. She also confirmed that her husband was never at home at the time of the Ripper murders.

The inspector called on two of the foremost experts on insanity in London to examine the doctor. The doctor admitted that he had been unbalanced for years and there were times when he could not remember what he had done. On one occasion, he had found himself sitting in his rooms with blood on his shirt front. He attributed this to a nosebleed. On another occasion, he had found his face covered in scratches.

Searches were made in the house and a Scotch tweed suit, light overcoat and soft felt hat were found. These matched the clothes as seen in Lees' vision.

The doctor was shocked at the thought of being the Ripper. He expressed horror at the crimes and acted as if the murderer was another man. When convinced of his own guilt, he begged to be killed at once.

A medical commission was held and it emerged that the doctor had a dual personality – the good existed side by side with the bad. It emerged that even as a young medical student at Guy's Hospital in London he had displayed murderous tendencies. He delighted in torturing animals and had continued his sadism even into married life. His wife had once caught him holding a cat over a burning lamp and on another occasion he almost beat their four-year-old son to death after catching him killing a fly.

The physician was placed in a private insane asylum in Islington and given the name Thomas Mason, alias inmate No 124. To explain the disappearance of the doctor, a sham

Jack the Ripper with one of his victims.

funeral was arranged and an empty coffin was placed in the family vault in Kensal Green Cemetery.

So ends the account.

So what are we to make of it? It sounds impressive until we look into the facts behind the Ripper murders. In the narrative, it is stated that the killings took place over several years with the Ripper claiming 17 victims. In reality, the murders took place over a period of ten weeks in 1888 – the last being the murder of Mary Kelly on 9 November. Only five women are generally acknowledged as Ripper victims and none were murdered in Crown Court.

Three other women were once thought by some to have been Ripper victims – Martha Tabram in August 1888, Alice McKenzie in July 1889 and Frances Coles in February 1891. Tabram had been stabbed 39 times. McKenzie's throat had been stabbed twice and she had suffered cuts and scratches to her body. Coles had her throat cut but was not mutilated. Most students of the case now dismiss all three murders as Ripper crimes. However, it should be noted that several Ripper historians do believe that Tabram may have been the Ripper's first victim.

The vision of seeing a murder at 12.40am cannot be correct as none of the women were killed at this time. There is also no record of the Ripper leaving a message on a wall saying he would kill 20 and then give himself up. Nor is there any record of a postcard being sent to the police which states that he would remove the ears of the ninth victim. It should, however, be noted that a letter making such a threat was sent to the Central News Agency. It was dated 25 September 1888 and claimed to be from the killer.

Dear Boss,

I keep on hearing the police have caught me but they won't fix me just yet. I have laughed when they look so clever and talk about being on the right track. That joke about Leather Apron gave me real fits. I am down on whores and I shan't quit ripping them till I do get buckled. Grand work the last job was. I gave the lady no time to squeal. How can they catch me now. I love my work and want to start again. You will soon hear of me with my funny little games. I saved some of the proper red stuff in a ginger beer bottle over the last job to write with but it went thick like glue and I cant use it. Red ink is fit enough I hope ha. ha. The next job I do I shall clip the lady's ears off and send to the police officers just for jolly wouldn't you. Keep this letter back till I do a bit more work, then give it out straight. My knife's so nice and sharp I want to get to work right away if I get a chance. Good Luck.

Yours truly

Jack the Ripper

Don't mind me giving the trade name

PS Wasn't good enough to post this before I got all the red ink off my hands curse it. No luck yet. They say I'm a doctor now. ha ha

This letter was the first to bear the name Jack the Ripper but is completely different from the postcard supposedly sent to the police.

And what of Dr Howard who it was claimed had revealed Lees' involvement in tracking down the Ripper? He vehemently denied the story and wrote a letter to an English newspaper, *The People*, after they had repeated it with the provocative suggestion that the doctor should be made to answer for his breach of vow.

> *St George's Club,*
> *Hanover Sqr, W.*
> *Jany 26-96*
>
> *Sirs*
>
> *A number of persons have called my attention to 'A startling story' in your widely read 'The People' – May 19. 1895 directly charging me with 'the breach of vow' etc.*
>
> *In this publication my name is dishonourably associated with Jack the Ripper – and in such a way – as if true – renders me liable to show cause to the British Medical Council why my name with three degrees attached should not be expunged from the Official Register.*
>
> *Unfortunately for the Parties of the other part – there is not a single item of this startling statement concerning me which has the slightest foundation in fact.*
>
> *Beyond what I may have read in newspapers, I have never known anything about Jack the Ripper. I have never made any public statement about Jack the Ripper – and at the time of the alleged public statement by me I was thousands of miles distant from San Francisco where it is alleged I made it.*
>
> *In my absence from London this statement has passed uncontradicted so long that the damage has multiplied beyond private methods of correction.*
>
> *I am Yours Truly*
> *B. Howard*

The journalist behind the story wrote to Howard and admitted that he had based his report on the Chicago story. He apologised unreservedly and the matter was dropped.

Robert Lees remained silent. It has been suggested that he was unaware of the story as he was convalescing in St Ives, Cornwall. Lees' silence and the threat of legal action from Dr Howard ensured that the story quickly fizzled out.

Lees continued with spiritualism and wrote several books on the subject which he said had been dictated to him by spirit. He retired to Leicester in 1928.

The Ripper/Lees story was revived by the *Illustrated Leicester Chronicle* in 1929 when

Robert James Lees.

they published an article by Hugh Mogford in which Lees claimed to know the identity of Jack the Ripper but was sworn to secrecy. Even Sir Arthur Conan-Doyle was denied the Ripper's name when he asked Lees about the matter.

Lees died in 1931 and the story of Lees and the Ripper was again repeated in the *Daily Express*. Cyril Morton, a crime-writer for the paper, travelled to Leicester and offered Eva Lees £500 to reveal the identity of the Ripper. She refused as she did not want her father's death overshadowed by his association with the Ripper murders. Morton left empty-handed. The *Daily Express* then published the claim that Lees had dictated a 'secret document' to a friend who had been told not to reveal its contents until after his death. The friend had then placed it in the hands of the newspaper. The *Express* further stated that Lees' children had confirmed that a pledge of secrecy had been put on their father after his discovery of the Ripper's real identity. It was also reported that Eva Lees had spoken of her father receiving a privy pension for many years.

The article was clearly a rehash of the old Chicago story, including the claim that the murders went on for over a year and reached double figures. The Lees children, who had been residing with their father in Leicester at the time of his death, were furious at the publication of the story and demanded to know its source. The paper refused to co-operate. Eva Lees later spoke to the newspaper *Le Matin*. She said the whole matter was distasteful but did confirm that her father 'played some part' in the hunt for Jack the Ripper.

The story of Lees and the Ripper was often repeated in books and magazines over the next few decades. A former Scotland Yard detective, E.T. Woodhall, wrote of the case in his 1935 book, *Crime and the Supernatural*. He said that he had no proof of the story but claimed he had heard it repeated several times at the Yard. He was also convinced that it was true and boldly stated that a 'black-japanned box' in the archives of the Home Office contained papers revealing the true identity of Jack the Ripper.

The story was resurrected in 1970 by Dr Thomas Stowell who claimed in *The Criminologist* that Queen Victoria's physician, Sir William Gull, was suspected of being the Ripper after being seen in Whitechapel at the time of the murders. He further claimed that Caroline Acland, Gull's daughter, had told him of her mother being greatly annoyed when a medium and a policeman visited their home one night during the time of the Ripper murders. She recalled that Sir William had been questioned by them and had admitted to lapses of memory since suffering a stoke in 1887. He had also once found blood on his shirt. However, Stowell did not think Gull was the Ripper. He claimed that the Ripper was a distinguished patient of the doctor who was suffering from terminal syphilis of the brain. The blood on Gull's shirt was due to the doctor having examined this patient. Stowell only referred to his suspect as 'S' but clues in the article made it clear he was referring to Prince Albert Victor, Queen Victoria's grandson and the heir to the British throne.

The story was again repeated in 1976 by Stephen Knight in his book *Jack the Ripper: The Final Solution*. Knight claimed that the Ripper murders were carried out at the wishes of the Prime Minister, Lord Salisbury. The victims of Jack the Ripper were deliberately targeted as all were privy to a secret marriage between Prince Albert Victor and a Catholic commoner, Annie Elizabeth Crook. They had been silenced as they were trying to blackmail the government. Knight further claimed that the Masons were involved – some of the mutilations being supposedly based on Masonic rituals. He mentioned the Chicago newspaper of 1895, believing it to be based on fact, and wrote that Lees had told Emily Porter, his great-niece, of his involvement in the Ripper investigation. He went on to echo Stowell's claim that Lees had tracked down Sir William Gull. Knight, unlike Stowell, was convinced that Gull was Jack the Ripper. He also believed that the artist Walter Sicket acted as a lookout for Gull during the murders. To make matters even more complicated, a coachman called John Netley allowed the killings to take place in his cab!

The Masonic/government conspiracy theory was based on statements made to Knight by Joseph Gorman Sicket who claimed to be the illegitimate son of Walter Sicket. The book became a best-seller but was later discredited when Sicket admitted that he had invented the story of a government/Masonic plot. He later retracted his confession but the damage had been done and very few Ripper experts now believe his story.

Knight also makes reference in his book to a letter sent to the police in July 1889.

Dear Boss,
You have not caught me yet you see, with all your cunning, with all your 'Lees' with all your blue bottles
Jack the Ripper

Knight cited this as proof that Lees' involvement in the investigation was known at the time of the murders. Stewart P. Evans, a leading Ripper historian and author, examined the original letter and realised that Knight had misread the word 'Lees'. It actually read 'tecs' which is slang for detectives.

So is there any truth in the story that Lees helped catch Jack the Ripper? It has been seen that the original story as printed in the Chicago newspaper is riddled with errors. The author Melvin Harris looked into this and concluded that it was a joke started by journalists of the *Sunday Times-Herald* who were members of The Whitechapel Club. This organisation was based at the back of the *Times-Herald* building and specialised in spreading elaborate hoaxes. He also suggested that the article contained deliberate errors to alert knowledgeable readers to the hoax. Other historians have questioned this, claiming that The Whitechapel Club was disbanded a year before the Chicago article. It should be noted that another suggested source for the article is W.T. Stead, who knew Lees. He had visited Chicago in 1894.

It has been already noted that Lees remained tight-lipped when the story first appeared in the press. So did he have something to hide? Eva Lees always maintained that her father had been involved in the Ripper investigation. A gold cross in possession of the Lees' family is produced as evidence of this. It is said to have been presented to the medium by the grateful prostitutes of Whitechapel.

Cynthia Legh, who knew the medium from 1912, went on record in *Light*, the Journal of the College of Psychic Studies (autumn 1970), saying that Lees had told her a version of the story several times. According to Lees, Queen Victoria had given him her personal authority to help the police.

In this version of the story, Lees led officers to the home of a doctor whose wife held a position at court. The doctor was removed to an asylum and a fake funeral arranged. A beggar who died in London was buried in his place. Victoria requested that Lees remove himself from London for five years to prevent any rumours emerging of the Ripper being connected with someone at court. Lees was also granted a pension from the Privy Purse for his services.

The *Journal of the Society for Psychical Research* investigated the case in their July – August issue for 1949. The author, Dr Donald J. West, the then research officer for the SPR, spoke to Eva Lees who confirmed that her father had 'detected Jack the Ripper by psychic means'. She knew the identity of the Ripper but was not prepared to reveal his name since his descendants could suffer. She did, however, say that he was a well-known London surgeon and came from a titled family. His funeral had also 'created quite a stir'.

West searched the obituaries of *The Times* and also checked the medical journals of the time but could find no death of a prominent London doctor in the six months following the last Ripper killing of November 1888. As previously noted, Sir William Gull has been accused of being the Ripper. However, he died over a year after the death of the last Ripper victim. It should also be remembered that Gull was also in his early 70s at the time of the murders and had suffered a partial stroke in 1887. Consulting the descriptions of witnesses who may have seen the Ripper, they all point to a man in his 20s or 30s.

West also wrote to Scotland Yard regarding Lees' involvement in the Ripper investigation. They replied:

> *New Scotland Yard S.W.1*
> *17th March, 1949*

> *Sir,*

> *With reference to your letter of the 8th March, regarding the 'Jack the Ripper' murders, I am directed by the Commission to inform you that, according to the records in this office, there is no foundation for the newspaper stories that the murderer was known to the police, and traced through the aid of a medium.*

> *I am to add that there is no record of the person named James Lees to whom you refer in your letter.*

> *Signed,*
> *Secretary*

It should be noted that a Mrs Brackenbury, who worked for the Society, visited Scotland Yard in 1931 and discussed the Ripper murders with several CID officials, including one who had been the keeper of the criminal records since 1901. None of them had heard of Robert Lees or any other medium involved in the investigation. She also questioned an ex-inspector Wensley who had been a police constable in Whitechapel at the time of the murders. He had never heard of Lees but was sure that he would have heard of him if the police had used a psychic to solve the case.

West also contacted the Home Office to check the claim made by Woodhall that they held a file on Lees. The following reply was received:

> *Home Office*
> *Whitehall*
> *December 29th, 1948*

> *Sir,*

I am directed by the Secretary of State to refer to your letter of the 30th November about the nineteenth-century murderer known as Jack the Ripper and to say that there is no reference in the records in the Department to the statement said to have been left by a medium named Lees and that no such file as you mention appears to exist.

Signed,

C. S. Brown

It can now be seen that Lees' involvement in catching Jack the Ripper is based solely on an inaccurate article from 1895 and brief statements made by Lees himself, his daughter and Cynthia Legh of the *Light* journal. The Home Office file referred to by Woodhall in his book – if it ever existed – has vanished.

It has to be admitted that many police files on the Ripper were lost, stolen or destroyed over the years – as late as 1987 Ripper documents stolen from the police files were returned anonymously to Scotland Yard – and so we cannot definitely rule out the claim that a file containing material relating to Lees once existed. It also must be noted that a large amount of Queen Victoria's personal correspondence and journals were destroyed after her death as it was felt by members of her family their contents could prove an embarrassment if published. We can only guess if Lees, Jack the Ripper and Victoria's interest in spiritualism featured in these destroyed papers.

In 1986 Peter Underwood published a book, *Queen Victoria's Other World*, which provided convincing proof of Victoria's interest in spiritualism. The book also contained a chapter on Lees. Underwood acknowledged that Lees' connection to the Ripper was 'somewhat tenuous'. He also confirmed that he had seen Donald West's original notes concerning his visit to Eva Lees which formed the basis for the report published in the *Journal of the Society for Psychical Research*. The notes revealed that West believed many of her stories relating to her father were inconsistent. She would, for instance, say that her father had no connection to John Brown but then would speak of their association. West concluded that there was no proof for her claims and believed they were probably hysterical fantasies. Despite this, Underwood remained convinced that there was some truth to the Ripper/Lees story. He also believed that there may have been a cover-up on the part of the authorities.

It must now be acknowledged that the story of Robert James Lees and Jack the Ripper is riddled with inconsistencies and even falsehoods. All we can say for certain is that Lees personally claimed on more than one occasion to have helped police catch the man known to history as Jack the Ripper.

However, when it is all said and done, the only documentary evidence from 1888 which confirms the medium's interest in Jack the Ripper are three brief entries in his diary.

Tuesday 2ⁿᵈ October. Offered services to police to follow up East End murders – called a fool and a lunatic. Got trace of man from the spot in Berner Street. Wednesday 3ʳᵈ October. Went to City Police again – called a madman and fool. Thursday 4ᵗʰ October. Went to Scotland Yard – same result but promised to write to me.

It must be left to the reader to decide if the police did eventually write to Lees and accept his offer to help them in their search for Jack the Ripper.

CHAPTER EIGHTEEN
MORE TALES FROM A GHOST HUNTER'S NOTEBOOK

A THAMES MYSTERY

A ferry steamboat that once plied its trade between Greenwich and Westminster was the scene of a strange occurrence. A young man was using the ferry one summer day when he noticed a young lady with a black veil sitting apart from the other passengers. As the boat neared Westminster Bridge she sprang to her feet and jumped overboard, much to the man's shock. He immediately took off his coat and jumped in after her. He swam about for some time but could not find her and so returned to the steamer where he was helped back on board by some of the crew and passengers.

Westminster Bridge.

The captain did not seem surprised. *'You are the third person this week who has jumped in after that creature.'*

'What! Do you mean to tell me she was merely fooling? But what became of her? I could find no sign of her in the water.'

The captain replied, *'What becomes of her is more than I or anyone else can tell you.'*

'Are you inferring that she was something supernatural?' the young man asked in surprise.

The captain could suggest no other explanation and went on to explain that a girl fitting the exact description of the one the man had tried to rescue had committed suicide by throwing herself off the steamboat at the very spot where he had seen the woman jump in. She had haunted the vessel periodically every since.

Westminster Bridge is the scene of another haunting. Two or three shadowy men are seen aboard a boat which approaches the bridge and then passes under it. It always vanishes before emerging on the other side.

KENNY EVERETT

Kenny Everett was a much-loved UK DJ and television personality whose madcap humour is still fondly remembered by his many fans. He was once married to Lee Everett Alkin, the psychic and former singer, who had developed an interest in spiritualism after realising that she had gifts as a medium herself.

In 1972 the couple had several male friends visiting their Surrey home. After supper they decided to hold a séance using an upturned glass and letters of the alphabet.

They all sat down and put their fingers on the glass. Almost immediately, it began to move at an alarming speed. It finally settled down and began to spell out the full name of John, one of the guests. It then spelt out a girl's name and John revealed that he had been engaged to her but had recently broken it off.

John was naturally shocked as he thought the girl was very much alive.

Kenny Everett. (Figgis-West)

However, the girl insisted she had died that day at noon after gassing herself following a row with her mother. She went on to say that she still loved him and wished they had not parted. She also said she felt cold and even gave the name of the mortuary where her body was.

It was little wonder that the group decided to end the seance. Kenny later recalled that *'John had gone terribly white. If this was a joke he thought it in very bad taste. The fantastic thing is that none of us, apart from John, even knew the girl's name, let alone that she had been engaged to him.'*

Lee Everett gave John the phone to ring his ex-fiancée's number. Kenny later recalled in a magazine interview that he *'found out that every detail the glass had given about the girl was true. But no one in that room could have known'.*

Lee later wrote in her book *The Happy Medium* that that incident convinced Kenny that life after death was indeed a reality.

THE PHANTOM MANSION

Knighton Gorges, on the Isle of Wight, was one of the most imposing mansions on the island. However, its history was a tragic one. Hugh de Morville, one of the murderers of Thomas Beckett, hid there on 27 December 1170, along with his fellow partners in crime, Reginald FitzUrse, Richard le Breton and William de Tracy.

Sir Tristram Dillington MP, the owner in the 18th century, died in mysterious circumstances. On 7 July 1721, it is claimed that he committed suicide by drowning himself in a lake in the grounds of Knighton Gorges after running up gambling debts. His valet is said to have placed his corpse upon his horse, Thunderbolt, and drove it into the lake. He hoped to make his death look like a riding accident and thereby prevent the estate from being forfeited by the Crown. Sir Tristram's ghost now rides his equally ghostly horse each year on the anniversary of his death.

The manor was destroyed in 1821 by the last owner, George Maurice Bissett. It is said that he did this to prevent his daughter from inheriting the property. She had invoked his wrath by marrying a clergyman against his wishes. Only the gateposts now remain to remind us of this once magnificent building.

The mansion is said to reappear on New Year's Eve in all its former glory.

One New Year's Eve in the early 1920s a young man was touring the island. He was attracted by the gateposts, featuring fine heraldic beasts, and decided to ask at the house for shelter. As he made his way up the drive he heard the sounds of a carriage and horses hurtling towards him. He quickly threw himself to the ground to avoid being run over. The carriage rushed by and the man got to his feet, somewhat angry and shaken but

The entrance to the vanished mansion of Knighton Gorges. (Figgis-West)

fortunately unhurt. As he walked towards the house, he could hear the sounds of music and laughter. He knocked at the front door several times but received no reply. He then looked into the window of the drawing room and saw a fancy-dress party in full swing with everyone dressed in Georgian clothing. Unable to gain entry, the young man returned to the road and made his way to nearby Newchurch. He found a room for the night and told the family of his visit to the mansion. He was surprised to be told that the building had been knocked down over a hundred years ago with only a barn, the gateposts and overgrown orchard now remaining. He refused to believe them and asked one of the men to return with him in the morning to prove the truth of what he had seen.

The next day they returned to the mansion. The man was shocked to discover the gateposts in a ruinous state. The heraldic beasts had vanished and the drive was overgrown. Of the house, there was no sign.

SICK AT HEART

Hortense Mancini, the Duchess of Mazarin, was the mistress of Charles II. The fickle and wanton Charles finally tired of her and had her pensioned off with rooms in Richmond Palace. Here she formed a close friendship with Madame de Beauclair, the former mistress of Charles's brother, James. As age and infirmity took their toll, the two would naturally speak of the possibility of life after death. Both decided to make a pact in which the first to die would return to inform the survivor of the reality of a future state.

The duchess was the first to die. During her last hours, Beauclair reminded her friend of their pact and the duchess assured her that she would return. Within an hour of this conversation, she was dead.

Years passed and the duchess did not appear. This naturally made her friend despair of a life beyond this world.

HORTENSE MANCINI
Duchesse de Mazarin
Née à Rome, Morte à Chelsey en Anglet.^{re} le 2 Juil.1699.

She once told a friend of her pact with the duchess, speaking in bitter terms, *'Did she still exist, no matter where, she would most certainly have found some means of communicating with me. That she has not done so convinces me that she no longer exists and that there is no life after life.'*

Some months later this person found themselves visiting a mutual friend of Madame de Beauclair:

'We were just set down to cards, about nine o'clock in the evening, as near as I can remember, when a servant came hastily into the room and acquainted the lady I was with that Madame de Beauclair had sent to entreat she would come that moment to her, adding that if she desired ever to see her more in this world she must not delay her visit.'

The woman was suffering from a cold and after learning from the servant that Madame de Beauclair was well, refused. She did promise, however, to visit her in the morning. A second more urgent request was soon sent and this time it was accompanied by a casket containing Beauclair's watch and various items of jewellery which she wanted the lady to have in remembrance of their friendship. Both friends, now realising that something was amiss, rushed to the lady's apartments in Richmond where Madame de Beauclair, sitting in a chair and looking perfectly healthy, told them that her death was near.

Despite reassurances, nothing would convince her that she would not die that very night. A clergyman was sent for and the two waited outside as he provided spiritual comfort to their friend.

The pair were then readmitted and both noted that Madam de Beauclair seemed no longer troubled. She told them she was resigned to her fate and only desired to spend her last moments with them. She then admitted that she had seen the ghost of the Duchess of Mazarin that very day.

'I perceived not how she entered, but turning my eyes towards yonder corner of the room, I saw her stand in the same form and habit she was accustomed to appear in when living: fain would I have spoken, but had not the power of utterance. She took a little circuit round the chamber, seeming rather to swim than walk, then stopped by the side of that Indian chest, and, looking on me with her usual sweetness, said, "Beauclair, between the hours of twelve and one this night you will be with me." The surprise I was in at first being a little abated, I began to ask some questions concerning that future world I was so soon to visit; but, on the opening of my lips for that purpose, she vanished from my sight.'

The time was now almost 12. Madam de Beauclair suddenly cried out, *'I am sick at heart'* and within half an hour she was dead. The apparition's prediction had proved correct.

THE MIDNIGHT APPOINTMENT

Elliott O'Donnell once wrote of a friend, Basil N. Hill, who was an actor. He told O'Donnell of a very curious experience that he had once had in London. As an actor myself, I can assure you that acting is never a profession to guarantee a regular wage and Basil found himself, like so many actors, penniless and out of work. One night, he found himself on the Thames Embankment with suicide on his mind. As he looked into the dark waters someone tapped him on the shoulder. It was a fellow actor named Bert. He was also thinking of ending it all and the two wondered if drowning was painful and if they would be punished in the afterlife – if indeed there was one – for killing themselves. Unbeknown to them, a policeman had been watching them and now came over, '*Here's a bob for you, boys. It's all I can afford. Better that, however, than the river.*'

Basil asked how the policeman knew they were thinking of jumping in.

'*By your appearance,*' the policeman said, '*anyone like me, who is used to the Embankment, can always tell a real down and out. There are plenty of sham ones, but you two have the genuine desperate look, which usually means the river. Since I have been on this beat I've seen several suicides, and saved probably a score or more from jumping in. Get a bit of grub and something warm to drink with that money, and, maybe, your luck will turn in the morning.*'

Both men were touched by the policeman's kindness and promised to follow his advice. They decided to go to a coffee stall to buy some sandwiches and a drink. They also agreed to meet at Waterloo Bridge the following day at midnight and jump in if their luck had still not changed.

The two parted with Hill spending the night under Covent Garden arches. The following morning he bumped into a friend, another actor, who had just won a part in a touring company.

His friend told him that they were looking for someone to play a parson, a part he felt Hill would be perfect for. His friend then lent him some money to smarten himself up before auditioning for the role. Hill was successful and was offered a bed at his friend's digs. The two were celebrating when Hill suddenly remembered his pledge to Bert. He made his excuses and rushed to the bridge to tell his friend of his good fortune. He arrived late, it was quarter past 12, and Bert was nowhere to be seen. He waited for some time but then concluded that Bert must have had some luck himself and had decided not to go after all.

The next evening Hill went to the Aquarium, a well-known place of entertainment in the City, to meet another friend. He was wandering about when he spotted Bert standing in the entrance to a side-show. His friend was staring at him intently. Hill walked over to ask

Waterloo Bridge.

how he was, but as he approached him his friend suddenly vanished. A few minutes passed and Hill again saw Bert in another part of the hall. Bert was again staring at him intently. This time he beckoned to him. Hill walked towards him but his friend disappeared.

Hill was somewhat puzzled by all this and wondered if he was hallucinating. He then bumped into his other friend and the two left the hall. You can imagine Hill's surprise when Bert suddenly walked by him, turning to stare as he did.

Hill dashed after him, but he vanished again. A feeling of eeriness now come over him and, returning to his friend, he started to shake. His friend asked why he looked so scared. Had he seen a ghost? Hill replied, '*Yes, it undoubtedly was a ghost.*'

The next morning Hill went into a library and looked through the newspapers. One headline caught his eye – '*Man's body found in the Thames*'.

The report stated that a man had been seen to jump from Waterloo Bridge at midnight. The tragedy had occurred on Monday night – the same day and time as his appointment with Bert. The report went on to state that the body had been found in the mud and had been identified as an out-of-work actor.

ST MARK'S EVE

It was believed that the spirits of those destined to die over the coming year appeared in churchyards on New Year's Eve and St Mark's Eve, the latter being on 24 April. To see the ghosts you had to sit in the porch of the church for three hours from 11pm. You had to do this for three successive years. On the third year you would see the spirits walk up the path and enter the church.

Those fated to die first would be at the front of the procession, those destined to live out most of the year would be the last to enter the church. It was considered dangerous to fall asleep during the vigil – to do so would invite your own death within a year.

One such attempt to test this belief occurred in the 19th century in the neighbourhood of Kilncote in Leicestershire. Two young men went to their local churchyard in secret on two successive St Mark's Eves. Nothing happened, and on the third year the pair found themselves once again in the churchyard.

It was a bright moonlit night and everywhere was still. It was long past midnight when suddenly they heard the tapping of high heels. The men strained their eyes to see who was coming and were soon rewarded by the sight of a girl in white walking towards the churchyard. She drew nearer and they noticed that she was wearing a dark shawl and a sunbonnet which concealed her face, of which only a few golden curls could be seen.

The boys were excited to discover that the tradition was true and watched eagerly as she made her way through the gate and into the churchyard. As she neared the church porch her features became visible. '*Good God, Bill*,' one of the men cried out. '*It's Bella!*' Bella was the man's sister.

The figure showed no sign of being aware of them and passed through the door into the church. The churchyard gate was then heard to click and another figure came into view. This time it was that of a middle-aged woman dressed in black. Her face was hidden by a handkerchief held close to the face. George, the man who had spoken before, thought her walk and appearance looked familiar, '*Oh God, my mother. Let's go, I can't bear to stay here any longer*,' he cried.

The pair decided to flee but as they did so, the gate clicked again and the apparition of a young man dressed in a cheap suit hurried up the path. On seeing it George fainted. It was his double.

A few months passed and an epidemic broke out in the village. Among the victims were George, Bella and their mother.

CHAPTER NINETEEN
THE BLACK CAT OF KILLAKEE

A few miles to the south of Dublin can be found Montpelier Hill (*Cnoc Mount Pelier*) and the ruins of a lodge used by the notorious Hell Fire Club in the 18th century. The building formed part of the Killakee estate and was owned by the Conollys, one of the most powerful families in 18th-century Ireland. One member, William, became speaker of the Irish House of Commons, and died leaving an annual income of £17,000. It was little wonder that he was regarded as the richest man in Ireland by his contemporaries.

William expanded the Killakee estate and in 1725 constructed a hunting lodge on the slopes of Montpelier Hill. A prehistoric cairn was partly destroyed to make way for the building, some of the stones being used in the new structure. Shortly after it was completed, a storm blew the roof off. Locals blamed the Devil for this and saw it as a punishment for disturbing the ancient burial chamber.

William Conolly died in 1729 and his successor allowed the lodge to be used by Richard Parsons, the 1st Earl of Rosse. Parsons was a member of the Freemasons and a notorious

Hellfire Club building. (Figgis-West)

The Dublin Hell Fire Club.

libertine. In 1737 he co-founded the Dublin Hell Fire Club with two friends after hearing about Sir Francis Dashwood's notorious Hell Fire Club in England. Parsons and his friends soon surrounded themselves with like-minded individuals and it was not long before tales of gambling, drinking, prostitution, Devil worship and even murder became linked with their meetings in the Eagle Tavern in Dublin and the lodge on Montpelier Hill.

It was claimed that at each gathering an empty chair was left for the Devil. A black cat was sometimes placed on the chair in honour of Satan and one of these unfortunate animals was once soaked in whiskey and set alight by Parsons in a sickening act of cruelty.

Another story tells of a priest who unexpectedly came to the lodge one night and found Parsons and his friends about to sacrifice a black cat. The priest grabbed the animal and uttered an exorcism, causing a demon to flee from it.

It is also claimed that at least one human sacrifice was performed by the members. A local dwarf with a misshapen and enlarged head was allegedly beaten and smothered to death. His body was then hidden on the estate.

Another tale alleges that Parsons and his cronies were playing cards when a mysterious black-suited stranger arrived and joined the game. One of the players dropped a card and, upon bending down, noticed that the man had cloven hoofs. The stranger realised that his identity had been discovered and vanished in a ball of flame.

Duals were also fought by members and at least three deaths occurred at Killakee as a result of this practice. The ghost of one of these men is still said to haunt the hillside.

The lodge burnt down in strange circumstances. It was alleged that the building was destroyed in an act of revenge after the Conolly family, sickened by the activities of the club, refused them a further lease on the building. Another version claims that one of the footmen accidentally spilt wine on Richard Chappell Whaley, one of the revellers. The man was so outraged that he threw brandy over the servant and set him alight. The fire quickly spread with several members of the club perishing in the flames. Whaley escaped through a window.

Following this, the club was forced to hold meetings in the nearby Stewards House. The building was originally a two-storey hunting lodge and dated from the 1760s. It later became a dower house (for use by the widow of the estate-owner) and also as a residence for the agent who managed the Killakee Estate.

Parsons died in 1741 and the Hell-Fire Club was disbanded. Whaley's son Thomas decided to revive the club in 1771. This new version was known as The Holy Fathers and lasted for another 30 years. Another murder was alleged to have been committed when a local farmer's daughter was kidnapped and tortured to death by Whaley. She was then cooked and eaten.

The Connolly family sold the estate in 1800 to Luke White, a bookseller and politician, who built a mansion across the road from the lodge. In the 1880s the estate passed through inheritance to the Massey family. However, the fortunes of the family declined and Hugh Hamon Charles, the 8th Baron Massey, was declared bankrupt and evicted from the main house in the 20th century. He was forced to live in the Stewards House before moving into a gatekeeper's lodge. He died in 1958.

In the 1920s the mansion was rented to the Countess Constance Markievicz, the 'Red Countess'. She was a staunch Irish nationalist, suffragette and the first woman to be elected to the House of Commons but declined to take her seat on political grounds. During her time at Killakee, five members of the IRA were shot dead during a gun battle on the estate.

Death returned to the estate again in 1931 when Rupert Young, a student from Trinity, was killed by members of the IRA guarding an explosives dump near the house. The building was then used by the Dublin Metropolitan Division of the Garda Siochana as a base from where they could investigate the murder and combat 'irregular military activities' in the area.

The mansion was sold to a builder in 1941 and demolished. In 1968 Stewards House was bought by Mrs Margaret O'Brien and her husband Nicholas and converted into an arts centre. Mrs O'Brien soon became aware of stories of a black cat, the size of an Airedale dog, which locals claimed had been haunting the area for at least 50 years.

It was not long before Mrs O'Brien began to see 'a big black animal' disappearing into the thick undergrowth of the garden. However, she thought little of it and concentrated on making the building ready for opening as a centre for Irish arts and crafts. In March 1968 Tom McAssey, an artist from Dublin, and two colleagues were decorating the house. They were working on the stone-flagged front hall.

He later told an Irish reporter about what had happened:

'I had just locked the heavy front door, pushing a 6-inch bolt into its socket. Suddenly one of the two men with me said that the door had opened again. We turned, startled. The lock was good and the bolt was strong, and both fastened on the inside.

We peered into the shadowed hallway, and then I walked forward, and sure enough, the door stood wide open, letting in the cold breeze. Outside in the darkness, I could just discern a black-draped figure, but could not see its face. I thought someone was playing a trick and said: 'Come in. I see you.' A low guttural voice answered: 'You can't see me. Leave this door open'.

The men standing behind me both heard the voice but thought it spoke in a foreign language. They ran. A long-drawn-out snore came from the shadow, and in panic, I slammed the heavy door and ran too. Halfway across the gallery I turned and looked back. The door was open again and a monstrous black cat crouched in the hall, its red-flecked amber eyes fixed on me'.

McAssey painted a picture of the cat which was then displayed in the house.

Killakee House. (Figgis-West)

In the nearby woods lived Val McGann, a former Irish pole vault champion, and now a painter. He too had seen a large cat.

'The first time I saw it, it frightened me stiff but on subsequent occasions, I have been more interested and amazed at the size of the beast. It is about the size of a biggish dog, with terrible eyes, I've even stalked it with my shotgun, but have never been able to corner it.'

Over the next few months, the sightings continued. McAssey again saw a shadowy figure standing in the main hallway. Locked doors were found to open by themselves and the cat was again seen in the building even when locked and bolted. Two workmen also saw what they thought was a nun standing in the former ballroom. She was standing in the middle of the room with her back to them but vanished as they approached her.

Mrs O'Brien now decided to call in a Catholic priest, who agreed to perform a service of exorcism in the house. This appeared to bring peace to the building and for a year all was quiet.

In October 1969 several Irish showbiz personalities – including singer Danny Doyle and comedian Noel Ginnity – asked Mrs O'Brien if they could hold a séance in the house. A stage conjurer was included to rule out any trickery on the part of the residents.

The group decided to use a Ouija board. The séance started and the glass was seen to spell out the words 'Pat Foster' and 'Go home, there is danger'. They then asked what the danger was and the glass spelt out the words 'lights'. The lights in the room then suddenly dimmed and those in the courtyard went out completely. A check could find no reason for the fault – bulbs and wires were in working order.

The Black Cat of Killakee.

Two days later the activity started to become more pronounced. Knocks were heard and lights started to switch themselves on and off in rapid succession. Doorbells were also heard despite the bells having been removed years before. Once, they rang all night.

The residents now found that sleeping at night was impossible, even on nights with no activity – a sense of uneasiness now filling the air. Four days after the séance, loud crashes were heard and it was found that large items of furniture had been thrown about – even those kept in locked rooms. A mediaeval oak chair had been taken apart joint by joint. Brass tacks that had held a tapestry in place on it were found placed in rows. Another chair was found smashed to pieces. Crockery and bottles were also found broken and paintings torn into thin strips.

The local milkman was asked to leave deliveries of milk in a nearby stream as Mrs O'Brien had no fridge. It was found that all the tinfoil tops had been removed but the milk was untouched. No trace of the foil could be found and Mrs O'Brien thought that birds could be responsible. She decided to build a stone box with a slate lid which was placed in the stream. Despite this, the caps continued to vanish.

Knitted children's caps, some new, others worn and dirty, also began to appear in the house itself. Some were found hanging on picture hooks or the back of doors. Sometimes coins were found inside them. Rosary beads would also appear from nowhere.

On another occasion, Mrs O'Brien was alone in the house as her husband was away on a trip to Cork. She was woken in the night by loud crashes coming from the ground floor. A search revealed nothing out of place and she could find no reason for the disturbance.

The art gallery seemed to be a focus for the haunting, and once Mrs O'Brien saw an unknown Eurasian man walking through the gallery in broad daylight. She approached him but found that he had disappeared. Another time, she saw two nuns walking through the same area. They too vanished on being approached.

A medium from Antrim, Shelia St Clair, was called to the house in 1970. She was joined by an Irish TV crew who filmed her as she made 'contact' through automatic writing with two 'nuns' – Blessed Margaret and Holy Mary. They had acted as servants in Satanic rituals held in the house during the time of the Hell Fire Club. The medium felt that much of the paranormal activity was due to evil forces released as a result of the rituals held there.

Another exorcism was held in July 1970 and, apart from odd knocks at night, this seemed to bring relative calm to the house. In 1971 a grim discovery was made when new plumbing was being laid in the kitchen. A shallow grave was found to contain the brass statue of a horned devil thumbing its nose. Further digging by the plumber revealed the skeleton of a human being with an enlarged head – the legend of the murdered dwarf had been no legend after all. A priest was called in and a burial service was held for the unfortunate victim. After this, the knocking sounds stopped.

Mrs O'Brien sold Killakee House six years later. In 1985, the new owner, Josef Frei, was interviewed on Irish television about the house which was now a restaurant. Although not experiencing anything himself, he confirmed that visitors often felt uneasy in the building, especially in a room adjacent to the bell tower – once used to call estate workers for their meals. This was the room where the body had been found. One South American visitor claimed to have seen a dwarf-like figure standing at the back of a room staring at her. She left immediately.

Killakee House is now a private residence again. The painting of the cat still hangs in the building. In 2015 members of the TV series *Ghost Adventures* visited the house to make a film about the hauntings there. They recorded unexplained footsteps, the meow of a cat, a woman's cry and even filmed a normal-sized black cat running from the house into nearby undergrowth. Shay Murphy, the owner, stated that he had never seen a black cat in the area before their visit. He also spoke of the time the house had been remodelled in June 2000. As a joke, the workmen decided to turn the painting of the phantom cat upside down. Within 15 minutes their power tools had suddenly begun turning themselves on and off. He also revealed that one winter's night he had seen a 'black cloud' moving towards him in one of the rooms. It had no discerning shape and vanished after passing through him.

Stewards House and the ruins of the lodge have now become something of a tourist attraction due to their reputation of being haunted. Indeed, many visitors claim to have seen figures or heard strange sounds in the vicinity of the ruined lodge. It appears that we have not heard the last of the Black Cat of Killakee or the evil legacy of the Hell Fire Club.

CHAPTER TWENTY
THROUGH A GLASS DARKLY

BY JASON FIGGIS

The Irish and ghost stories are culturally inextricably linked. There is a vibrant history of storytellers (Seanchaí) who would huddle their audience around campfires, in drawing rooms of great houses and in community buildings across the nation. Some of these tales have a recognisable plotline running throughout – with perhaps a few details reliably altered to indulge a local flavour.

But, having said that, many of these tales are also inextricably linked to particular landmarks and the details have remained unaltered over the ensuing centuries.

Marsh's Library in the nation's capital Dublin, rests up against the boundary wall of one of that city's great cathedrals – St. Patrick's. The library is approached through a narrow gate – ornately designed and wrought in iron and having negotiated a number of rather steep stone steps, a visitor is soon entering within the walls of its wood-panelled interior. It is atmospheric throughout, eerily quiet and even the venerable wooden floor declines to creak beneath the foot when you walk upon it.

This is Ireland's oldest free public library and is haunted by its founder, the impressively monikered Archbishop Narcissus Marsh (his brothers were given the names Epaphroditus and Onesiphorus). Born in Wiltshire, England, in 1638, Marsh became one of the first members of the Dublin Philosophical Society. He contributed an early paper to that Society, called 'An Introductory Essay on the Doctrine of Sounds, Containing some Proposals for the Improvement of Accousticks', in which he was apparently the first to use the word microphone.

While Marsh was Archbishop of Dublin and living as a bachelor in the Palace of St. Sepulchre he arranged for his niece, young Grace Marsh, to look after the housekeeping. Grace was only 19 and probably found the Archbishop's lifestyle and strict discipline rather depressing. On 10 September 1695, this rather sad entry appears in his diary: '*This evening betwixt 8 and 9 of the clock at night my niece Grace Marsh (not having the fear of*

Marsh's Library. (Figgis-West)

God before her eyes) stole privately out of my house at St. Sepulchre's and (as is reported) was that night married to Chas. Proby vicar of Castleknock (North Dublin) in a Tavern and was bedded there with him – Lord consider my affliction.' Marsh died in 1713 and is buried just outside his library, in the grounds of St. Patrick's Cathedral.

Grace is said to have left her distraught uncle a note concealed in one of the many thousand volumes lining the library shelves. He never found it. Bram Stoker – the author of one of the most famous of all novels of gothic horror, *Dracula* – who studied books at the library on several occasions – heard many a story of the ghostly figure of the Archbishop walking among the great towering shelves, which stretch from floor to ceiling, his shadowy fingers retrieving book after book, in search of the note which he never found in life.

Grace Marsh lived to be 85 years old.

Another fascinating landmark is the austere and supremely impressive Leap Castle in Co. Offaly (some 135km from Dublin). There are several ghosts associated with this building which – having stood as backdrop to the many bloody battles of warring Chieftains – it is hardly surprising.

It is thought to have been built in the 13th century by the O'Bannon clan and originally called 'Leap of the O'Bannons'. The O'Bannons were the 'secondary chieftains' of the territory and were subject to the ruling O'Carroll clan. There is evidence that the castle was constructed on the same site as an ancient stone structure perhaps ceremonial in nature, and that the area has been occupied consistently since the Iron Age (500 BC), but possibly since Neolithic times.

Leap Castle. (Figgis-West)

Castle Leslie. (Figgis-West)

Leap Castle lays claim to being the most haunted castle in Ireland and the early 20th century discovery of at least 150 human skeletons, buried in its foundations, adds easy veracity to this claim.

The wife of a recent owner of the impressive structure is said to have awakened many of the spirits dwelling at the castle, through the practice of seance with the most terrifying being that of a pale woman, dressed in red and brandishing a dagger in an acutely threatening manner. The castle's Bloody Chapel is reputed to be its most haunted area and fills regularly with brilliant white light in the pitch black of night.

This brings me to an episode when I collaborated on the Discovery Civilisations feature documentary *The Twilight Hour*, with the celebrated photographer Sir Simon Marsden. We travelled as guests of Sir John Leslie to his magnificent ancestral home 130km north of Dublin – Castle Leslie – where Simon was to photograph some extraordinary rooms of the castle, which had fallen into neglect.

The castle is fashioned in the Scottish Baronial style and was designed by the firm of Lanyon, Lynn and Lanyon in 1870 for Sir John Leslie, 1st Baronet, MP. It is situated where an earlier castle stood but never had a defensive purpose.

I filmed Simon at a distance to allow him the necessary concentration to capture what he is famous for – magical black and white images (shot on InfraRed film). But it was not long before he invited me to look through the lens at one of his subjects. He asked me what I saw and, apart from the beautiful composition, I remarked that there was a strange dancing light gambolling in the lens. He agreed and went on to tell me that never, in his 40-year career as a professional photographer, had he experienced anything even remotely similar.

We also agreed that the strange light was not visible in the room – at least to the naked eye. It appeared that Simon's camera had the facility to harness what we could not. A few months later I revisited the faded grandeur of the ballroom where Simon and I had worked together, this time with my father, Peter.

In a fit of daring, we decided to walk the length of the hall and into the ballroom at midnight – without the aid of a torch. When we arrived in the space where Simon and I had had our experience, my father and I stood still and embraced the serenity as we observed the shadows stretch across the broad surface of the floor from the moonlight cast from beyond a thin aperture in the shutters. Suddenly, the entire room lit up with a great white light, brilliant and searing in its intensity but, as soon as it had appeared, it was gone, plunging us back into darkness. Accompanying this phenomenon was a strange depressive atmosphere and my father and I withdrew quickly and out into the fresh air that the cool night afforded us.

We never did discover the source or indeed if anyone else had experienced similar, but I could not help feeling that this experience and the strange dancing light in the lens of Simon's Nikon were somehow connected.

FINALLY ...

John Aubrey, the 17th-century English biographer, folklorist and antiquary, took more than a passing interest in the supernatural. The following note is taken from his Miscellanies (1696).

'Anno 1670, not far from Cirencester, was an apparition: being demanded, whether a good spirit or a bad? returned no answer, but disappeared with a curious perfume and most melodious twang. Mr W. Lilly believes it was a fairy.'

ABOUT THE AUTHOR

John West was born in Edmonton, London. He now lives in Suffolk. He is a film producer, actor, award-winning DJ and TV presenter and is the author of books and articles on history, crime, ghosts and folklore. One of his guides, Roman Lincoln, was turned into a BBC Radio Lincolnshire documentary. Other books include studies of Roman York, Oliver Cromwell and Victorian murders. His first book on British ghosts – *Britain's Haunted Heritage* – was published by JMD Media in November 2019.

As a journalist, John has written for magazines including *Psychic News* and *Suffolk and Norfolk Life*. His features have ranged from celebrity interviews to investigations of famous hauntings from the UK and beyond.

He has worked as a presenter at six radio stations, including BBC Radio Suffolk, and has several hundred shows to his credit.

John was Mustard TV's regular studio historian for over three years and appeared on the Norfolk station to talk about subjects ranging from the Romans to The Beatles. He was also a guest on London Live TV where he discussed the photographer and author Simon Marsden and Jason Figgis's film about his life and work.

John was a supporting artist on BBC's *Detectorists*, Netflix's *The Crown*, and feature films *The Personal History of David Copperfield*, *Grandest Wedding of Royals* and Danny Boyle's *Yesterday*.

He has been interviewed on BBC Cornwall, BBC Essex, BBC Norfolk, BBC Suffolk, BBC Lincolnshire, KCOR Radio, RWSfm, Felixstowe Radio, Felixstowe TV, Blythe Radio, Siren Radio, ICR, Deben Radio, Blog Talk Radio, IO Radio and Minster FM about his books and his interest in history, film and folklore. He has been the subject of articles in several newspapers and magazines concerning his books and interest in ghosts and history.

In 2018 John teamed up with film and TV writer/director Jason Figgis. He became a producer/publicist on the film *Simon Marsden: A Life in Pictures*, going on to produce and act in Figgis' M.R. James inspired chiller Winifred Meeks. Other productions from the team include *The Grey Man*, *Clare Island*, *The Wedding Ring*, *In Our Day*, *Mythmaker: George A. Romero*, *The Black Widow* and *Dunkirk 80*. Several other film and documentary projects with Figgis are now in pre-production.

John is also a photographer with work featured in newspapers and magazines across the UK. His first photographic exhibition was held in Suffolk in 2017.

RECOMMENDED READING

Chapter One – The Mystery of Jimmy Garlick
Haunted London (1973) Peter Underwood

Chapter Two – The Haunting of Rattlesden Rectory
The World's Strangest Ghost Stories (1955) R. Thurston Hopkins

Chapter Three – Brother Ignatius
A Host of Hauntings (1973) Peter Underwood

Chapter Four – York: Britain's Most Haunted City
Ghosts Of An Ancient City (1996) John V. Mitchell

Chapter Five – The Spectres of Edinburgh Castle
Haunted Edinburgh (2007) Alan Murdie

Chapter Six – Welsh Phantoms
Haunted Wales (2010) Peter Underwood

Chapter Seven – The Kersey Enigma
Adventures in Time (1997) Andrew MacKenzie

Chapter Eight – London's Haunted Churches
Ghosts of London (1975) Jack Hallam
Haunted London (1973) Peter Underwood

Chapter Nine – A Most Curious Haunting
Ghosts and Witches (1954) James Wentworth Day
Phantom Footsteps (1959) Alisdair Alpin MacGregor

Chapter Ten – Royal Ghosts
Haunted Royal Homes (1987) Joan Forman

Chapter Eleven – Lincoln's Haunted Heritage

Haunted Lincoln (2009) David Brandon

Ghosts of Lincoln (1995) Jenny Bright & Dr David Cross

Chapter Twelve – Scotland's Road of Horror

Gazetteer of Scottish and Irish Ghosts (1973) Peter Underwood

Chapter Thirteen – Tales From a Ghost Hunter's Notebook

The World's Strangest Ghost Stories (1955) R. Thurston Hopkins

The Haunted Homes and Family Traditions of Great Britain (1897) John Ingham

A Ghost in The Isle of Wight (1929) Shane Leslie

Ghosts Over Britain (1977) Peter Moss

A Secret History (2001) Alistair Taylor

Chapter Fourteen – The Devil and Major Weir

Edinburgh: City of the Dead (2004) Jan-Andrew Henderson

Chapter Fifteen – The Ghosts of St Albans

Haunted St Albans (2013) Paul Adams

Ghosts of Hertfordshire (1994) Betty Puttick

Chapter Sixteen – Scottish Tales of Terror

Ghosts Over Britain (1977) Peter Moss

Scottish Ghost Stories (1911) Elliott O'Donnell

The Ghost Book (1955) Alisdair Alpin MacGregor

Chapter Seventeen – Catch Me When You Can: Robert James Lees and the Hunt for Jack the Ripper

Queen Victoria's Other World (1986) Peter Underwood

Chapter Eighteen – More Tales From a Ghost Hunter's Notebook

The Happy Medium (1983) Lee Everett

Ghosts of London (1932) Elliott O'Donnell

Ghosts of Hampshire and the Isle of Wight (1983) Peter Underwood

Chapter Nineteen – The Black Cat of Killakee

Haunted Dublin (2008) Dave Walsh

Further Reading

Haunted Castles (1974) Marc Alexander

The Good Ghost Guide (1994) John Brooks

A Ghost Hunter's Game Book (1958) James Wentworth Day

Our Haunted Kingdom (1973) Andrew Green

Ghost Stations (1986) Bruce Barrymore Halpenny

The Ghost Hunter's Road Book (1968) John Harries

Haunted Houses (1907) Charles G. Harper

Railway Ghosts and Phantoms (1989) W. B. Herbert

Ghosts Over England (1953) R. Thurston Hopkins

Dangerous Ghosts (1954) Elliott O'Donnell

Phantoms of the Night (1956) Elliott O'Donnell

This Haunted Isle (1986) Peter Underwood

Britain's Haunted Heritage (2019) John West

The Penguin Book of Ghosts (2008) Jennifer Westwood & Jacqueline Simpson

The Occult (1971) Colin Wilson

Poltergeist! (1981) Colin Wilson

ND - #0317 - 270225 - C0 - 234/156/11 - PB - 9781780916170 - Gloss Lamination